THE ART OF BODY SINGING

CREATE YOUR OWN VOICE

VOLUME I
ALL LEVELS

by
Breck Alan

Dedicated to Robert Cord

Produced by Breck Alan
Executive Produced by Wendy Rubin
Recorded and engineered by Breck Alan at Your Voice Vocal Studio, Austin, Texas
(with borrowed equipment from Charles Reeves & Scottie Closter)
Sound Recording Edited by Charles Reeves & Breck Alan at Chicky's, Austin, Texas
Text Edited by Troy Reust, Bethany Siegler & Wendy Rubin, Book Layout by Wendy Rubin
Additional graphic design by Lindsay Holmes
Illustrations by Peggy Pellett, pg. 32 postcard designs by Robin Borgers,
Cover concept by Breck Alan, Cover illustration by Erica Vhay,
Photography by Wendy Rubin
Sound recording segues 1. Airport Jive 2. Circus Trip 1 , 2 & 3. Weird Rain and 4. Tiny's Tim
Written by Charles Reeves and Breck Alan Copyright 1996
All song examples in "The Art of Body Singing" written by Breck Alan
The Art of Body Singing, Volume 1 text and recorded material written by Breck Alan.
Copyright 1997,

Second edition 2001, Original printing 2000
The title "The Art of Body Singing"TM Breck Alan
For more information and to purchase Volumes II - IV of this system, please contact:
joe's production & grille, inc.
4919 N. Broadway, Warehouse 22,
Boulder, Colorado 80304
Toll free: 1.888.joesgrille (1.888.563.7474)
www.bodysinging.com
www.breckalan.com
breck@joesgrille.com

Published By Breck Alan Music/Snacky Time Records, Boulder, Colorado
Volume 1 ISBN 0-9705382-1-9
Library of Congress Control Number: 2001012345

Contents
Create Your Own Voice: Volume I

Introduction

The Art of Body Singing treats the serious student of voice to a meticulous, well organized journey, centered around the mechanics and techniques necessary in high performance singing. Body Singing adheres to the same essentials that any fine instrument-maker swears by: high quality design, high quality materials, and high quality assembly. Thus, the first concept of Body Singing: the voice is an instrument, assembly required. The system offers a methodical approach to vocal training, incorporating both classical and contemporary techniques. It is designed to teach proper vocal hygiene, high performance singing skills, personal style development and a professional outlook for ongoing growth long after leaving the teacher's side.

Most systems of vocal training, both historically and currently, are oriented in a coaching fashion, where students begin singing right away and are given only the vaguest tips on how to improve technically. And while there can certainly be a lot to learn from a coaching situation, i.e. repertoire training, sight reading, performance skills etc., these subjects can not be compared to vocal mechanics training. In the past, the only place to get really decent vocal mechanics training was from a good opera program. The drawback being you received training via a style, and that usually meant no matter what type of music you might later sing, you would probably sound like an opera singer trying to sing something else.

So what's the answer? The answer is a high level system of vocal training based on technique and not style. A system based on the ear as the first component of the voice, and then linking the ear to the series of physical feelings connected with producing sound from the body. The result being your own personal style of singing vs. singing on auto-pilot using muscle memory or pure imitation as the outcome of song coaching.

There is a lot of information and mis-information in the world concerning voice production. I have personally trained with some of the best vocal trainers, and some of the worst. I have spent countless hours with the more notorious published systems of voice as well as some of the least noteworthy. I have spent many a late night experimenting with techniques in search of that "Holy Grail Tone." So, after twelve years of singing, both as a student and as a professional, I set out to structure a system for vocal training. I truly wanted to create a balanced system incorporating the most effective information I had learned or discovered along my journey. Over five years later, the result is *The Art of Body Singing*. My belief is that I can literally save a student several years in their attempts to clearly understand the instrument called voice.

I must also credit my experience in the martial arts as much of my influence in structuring *The Art of Body Singing*. Good martial arts' systems are taught from the ground up and add bit by bit to a solid foundation of learning. *The Art of Body Singing* borrows this systematic method of teaching and is designed for all levels of singers. Beginners will enjoy the fact that *The Art of Body Singing* starts literally at the beginning and clearly outlines how the instrument works in everyday terminology. Advanced singers will be ecstatic as they discover clear answers to the often glossed over questions of voice, while learning to use effective tools to conquer the brick walls they often come up against when trying to improve.

The voice like any other instrument is a lifelong pursuit; *The Art of Body Singing* will be an ongoing source of inspiration and information unlike any other in this world.

Truly Yours,

Breck Alan

INTRODUCTION TO VOLUME 1

Welcome to *The Art of Body Singing*. No matter what level of singer you are, this is where you want to begin with this program. If you have some experience, you may find yourself working quickly through the first two volumes. However, these are necessary volumes to establish the vocabulary and foundation to move on in this system we call "Body Singing." Ideally, you should work one subject at a time, first listening to the recorded program then reviewing that subject in the booklet. The two mediums have been created to compliment each other in this program and, when used together, should prove to be frightfully effective. Don't work too quickly. Stay on each subject until you feel that you have grasped its full purpose, and have memorized the exercise so that you can practice it without the accompaniment of the recording or an instrument.

One of the goals of this system is to teach your voice to become a self-sufficient, freestanding instrument. It might help you at first to make a separate tape of just the exercises from "Body Singing" in the order that they appear, so that you might have a quick reminder of how they sound for your practice and warm-up sessions. Due to the amount of information covered in *The Art of Body Singing*, the recorded examples are not as long as you'll want them to be for your practice and warm-ups. So just use them as your starting examples, stop the recording, and commit them to memory. It is also likely that the starting notes for many of these exercises won't be a perfect fit for everyone. Once again, just use the example to learn the exercise then move the starting note to a more comfortable position. There might be times when it will be easier for women to learn the exercise from the men's example (following along an octave higher) and for men to learn from the woman's example (following along an octave lower). If this is difficult for you to do at first, ask someone (a musician friend or a music teacher) to help you figure it out. Once you understand how to move one or two of the exercises, custom fitting the rest of them shouldn't be a problem.

The voice is an instrument, an acoustic instrument to be exact. And like any other acoustic instrument, the voice has very specific physical properties that make it tick. What is unique to the voice is that you cannot buy it off the shelf like any other instrument you wish to play, but must instead build the instrument yourself. The voice can not be explained so simply as "being a muscle that gets stronger the more it is used." The voice is not one thing, but instead several individual mechanical components inside your body. These components must be located, developed, and taught to work with the other components harmoniously. The voice is like playing an instrument in the dark...without any hands. Every sound you make with your voice is connected to a feeling, or rather a series of feelings inside your body. The goal with this system of voice training is to develop a deep connection with your instrument....your body...your voice.

FUNDAMENTALS

The Four Parts of the Voice:

The *four parts of the voice* form a perfect democracy. They consist of:

1. *The Inner Ear:* The subjects of The Inner Ear relate to musicianship (i.e. pitch, note choice, rhythm, etc.) and instrument specific recognition (i.e. tone, inflection, volume, attitude, etc.) Although a singer's musicianship is greatly enhanced by this program due to the methodology of its teaching, the primary focus of the first four volumes of this system is instrument specific recognition via mechanics and technique training. So, always remember, the first part of the voice is "The Inner Ear."

2. *The Throat:* Think of the throat as a big circle including the mouth, tongue, larynx (Adam's Apple) and all of the muscles and cartilages from the face down to the shoulders. The vocal cords are the beginning source of all actual sound from the voice. They are housed in the larynx and are surrounded by several muscles that can either greatly enhance their performance or greatly hinder it. This is such an important subject to grasp for both proper vocal hygiene and good tone production.

3. *Support System:* All of that which is connected with the control of breath, basically your entire torso, is what makes up your "support system." Breath is the fuel for tone production. Without fully controlled support in singing, interesting and varied tone production is severely restricted. It is also important to recognize that several of the vocal health problems that localize in the throat can be cured by proper breath support.

4. *Resonance:* The sympathetic vibrations of your entire body, intensifying the tiny vibrations started in the throat by the vocal cords, is the definition of resonance. Enough emphasis cannot be placed on how small the initial tone produced by the vocal cords is. Often called vocal folds these tiny mucosa-lined ligaments (the vocal folds actually consist of five layers of tissue with muscle tissue in the center) vibrate much like the strings of an acoustic instrument, at varying speeds, to produce the initial pitch and tone of the instrument (There are several studies as to the specific functions of the vocal cords, which we'll talk more about later, but for now just think of them as the strings to your instrument). The rest is left up to articulation in the mouth and resonance in the head and body. Just as with any great acoustic instrument resonance in voice production plays such an important role in the overall tonal characteristics that its cultivation cannot be overstressed.

THE STEREO ANALOGY OF THE FOUR PARTS OF THE VOICE

I like to compare the four parts of the voice to a stereo system. Through specific training your ear becomes the recorded material e.g. your CD collection. Your throat, being the first medium of sound production, can be compared to the

CD player. Your support system (breath) fuels the tone, and can be compared to the amplifier. And your body is the source of resonance and tone projection, and can therefore be compared to a speaker system.

BEFORE WE GET STARTED

For the Supposedly Tone Deaf

If you are already someone with a pretty good musical ear then please move on to "Getting Started." If, on the other hand, you are among the ranks of the "supposedly tone deaf," here's what you need to do before you get started with the program. You need to find, buy, or borrow a keyboard of just about any kind. An inexpensive kid's keyboard will work just fine, but of course a higher quality unit might make things even easier.

Right out of your speaking voice, I would like for you to count from one to ten. With each number sustain the vowel just a little longer (i.e. one, two..uuu, three...eeee, etc,) You are speaking these numbers on a pitch (a specific vibrating frequency, i.e., a C, C#, D, etc.). It is important here that you identify the pitch you are speaking on with a pitch on the keyboard. Try staying on the same pitch for now if you can. You may need someone to help you identify the pitch at first, but once you know the general area of your speaking voice, you should be able to match it to a note on the keyboard by yourself after a little while. Once you can do this, pick a vowel (a, e, i, o or u) and really hear yourself matching the pitch of that vowel with the pitch you are playing on the keyboard. Now begin descending one note at a time on the keyboard and following with your voice. After a few notes come back up to where you started and this time, ascend past it by a few notes. Repeat this exercise several times growing a little further each time. This may take you several days (or longer) until this becomes easy and consistent for you, but with patience it will pay off greatly. After this exercise is under your control, begin to move by two notes at a time (i.e. white note to white note with a black note in between) along with the keyboard. Once your ear can easily follow the keyboard around, you are ready to move on with the program. There will be more ear training later on, but this should be enough to get you started. I don't really believe in a "tone deaf" ear, just an uneducated and possibly, tired ear. So, be patient and gentle and your ear will wake up and grow right along with the rest of your voice.

GETTING STARTED

We start with the throat as it is the first mechanical component of the voice and the initial source of our tone. It is also the only part of the voice which physically suffers when we abuse it. You must master the art of a tension free throat to sing healthily and to realize the voice's maximum potential. A singer must first learn to completely relax the constrictor muscles in the throat. These are the muscles used to lower the epiglottis in swallowing so that food and water do not pass down the trachea, but instead down the esophagus. These muscles are so often used that their natural reaction is to over-react in the singing process. Most

ex. 1a

singers start out by trying to sing like a balloon. When we squeeze air out of a ballon, the tip vibrates creating a tone. The harder you squeeze the air and the closer you pinch the end of the balloon together, the higher the pitch of the tone. Yes, pitch and tone mean different things. Pitch is what note you play and tone is how it sounds. Our throat isn't a balloon. We need to keep our throat open so that the vocal cords can vibrate freely. By constricting the throat and using the additional air needed to create a higher pitch (the higher the pitch, the faster the vibration necessary by the vocal cords), we not only severely kill our tone, but we run the risk of over-pressurizing our vocal cords, which can result in serious vocal health complications. The tone dies because the throat is ultimately the tone passage and by constricting, we make that passage smaller which results in a skinnier overall tone. So be healthy and sound good, relax your throat. See diagrams 1a. and 1b on page 12.

ex. 1b

THE SEVEN POINTS OF RELAXATION

If you look at diagram # 1b, you will see how all of the muscles in your face, neck and throat are tightly intertwined. The purpose of the *Seven Points of Relaxation*, is to use your hands to loosen and relax these muscles from the "outside," so that the feeling of relaxation will grow to a deeper level "inside" your throat.

ex. 1c

1. *Down the Face (see ex. 1a):* Gently rub down the face with finger tips.

2. *Jaw Hinge (see ex. 1b):* Massage deeply at the jaw hinge in front of the ears, at the pressure point of the jaw directly under the earlobes, and warble (shake fairly vigorously) the cheeks.

3. *Stretch Jaw (see ex. 1c):* Using your index fingers and your thumbs, gently stretch the jaw downward and then back upwards to close your mouth. Do this a few times until you feel no resistance from the jaw hinge.

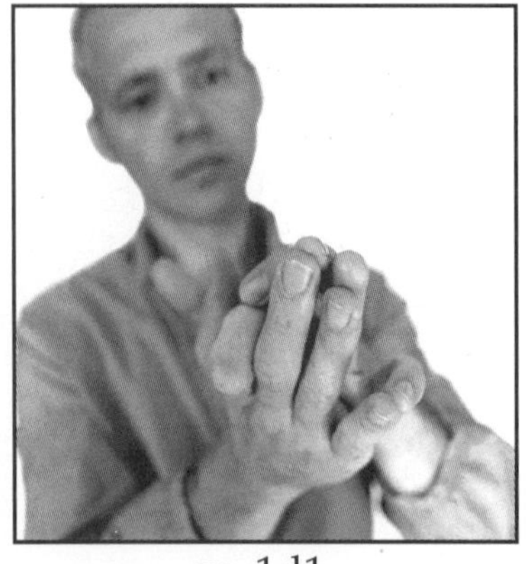
ex. 1d1

4. *Root of Tongue (see ex. 1d1, 1d2, 1d3):* Use these examples to align your fingers properly, then place your finger tips on the bottom of your chin. Move them back towards the throat until they slide up to the soft, spongy muscle that is the root of your tongue. Now swallow. The root of the tongue should stiffen up and push your finger tips down. If this happens, you are in the right place. Now with a piston action, alternating up and down with your fingers, massage this area. Singers with long fingernails might try wearing gloves of some kind to avoid any unnecessary discomfort. The goal is to get this area completely loose and relaxed. Practice talking on different pitches while massaging this area. Try to keep the root of your tongue completely soft and relaxed while you're talking on these different pitches. This is a key area to eliminate constriction in the throat during phonation (producing voice).

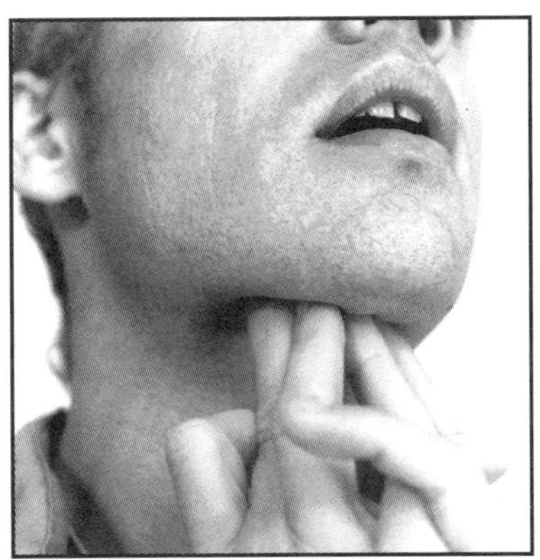
ex. 1d2

5. *Horizontal Larynx (see ex. 1e):* With your palms facing out, place your finger tips on the outside of the ligaments surrounding your larynx. If this is uncomfortable, try using the fingertips and thumb of one hand to move the larynx. Be careful to still keep your fingers on the outside of the ligaments surrounding the larynx. Never move the larynx by touching it directly. Keep your finger tips low so that you are not pushing on the glands under your jaw. Gently move your larynx side to side, pushing with one group of fingers, then the other. If you are feeling or hearing any clicking in the throat, this is do to built-in tension in the ligaments surrounding the larynx. Be gentle, this clicking should go away after your throat learns to relax. Don't push your larynx very far to either side, a little horizontal movement is all we need here. This will not only help loosen and relax this area, but will also stimulate some nice circulation as well.

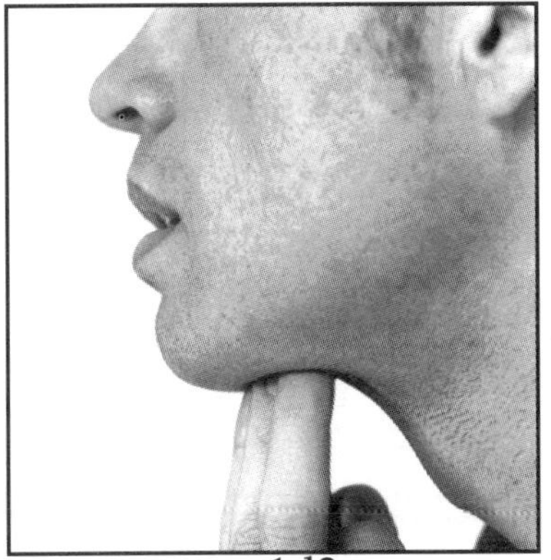
ex. 1d3

6. *Back of Head and Neck (see ex. 1f):* Imitating lobster claws with your fingers and thumbs massage the back of your head and neck. There is a nice pressure point at the base of the skull that should eliminate a lot of tension in your neck.

7. *Shoulders (see ex. 1g):* Also using the lobster claw hands, massage the muscles in your shoulders.

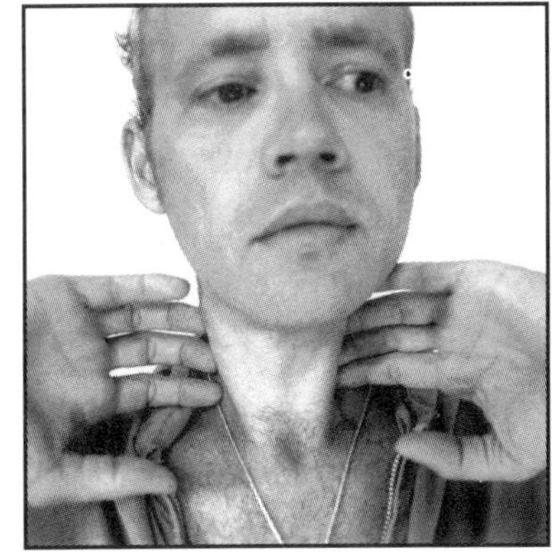
ex. 1e

DROOL EXERCISE

This is a throat relaxation and warm up exercise. The tangible result of this exercise is to be so relaxed in the throat so that you're stimulating the salivatory glands. This level of relaxation helps insure that the constrictor muscles in the throat will not interfere with comfortable and healthy singing (See diagram 1a to see how muscles connect). Really capture this feeling and learn to maintain it throughout your singing no matter how dynamic.

Listen now to example on **Volume One** recording.

If in doubt about the volume of this exercise, you're too loud. The *Drool Exercise* consists of the vowels "a," "e," "i," "o," and "u," preceded by the consonant "h" for a nice gentle entry into the note. Use the first five notes of the major scale in a very comfortable loca-

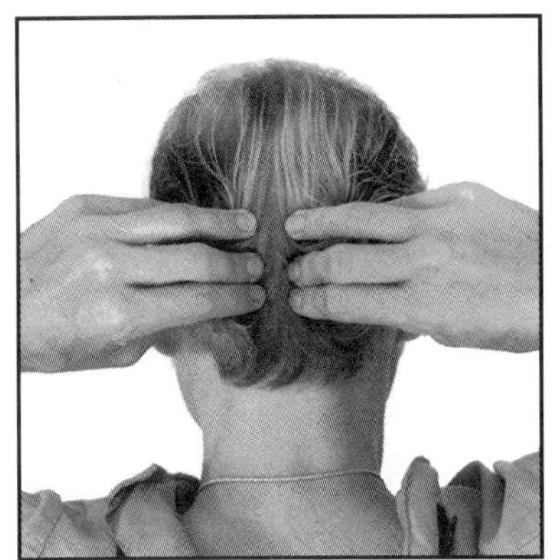
ex. 1f

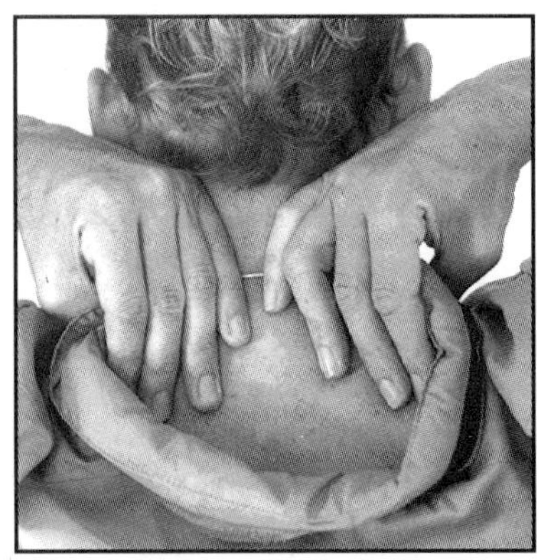
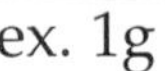
ex. 1g

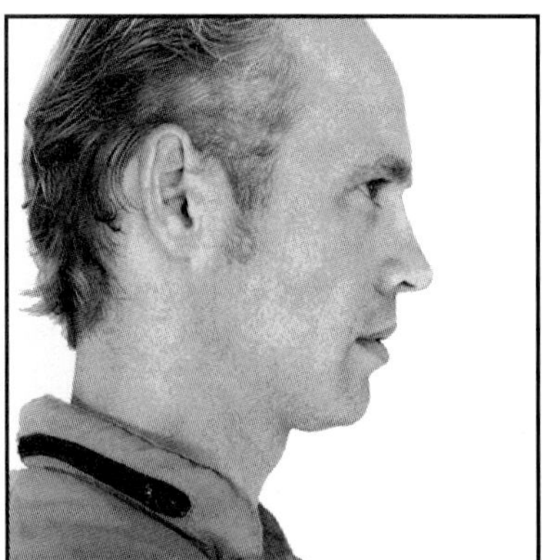
ex. 2a1 - correct

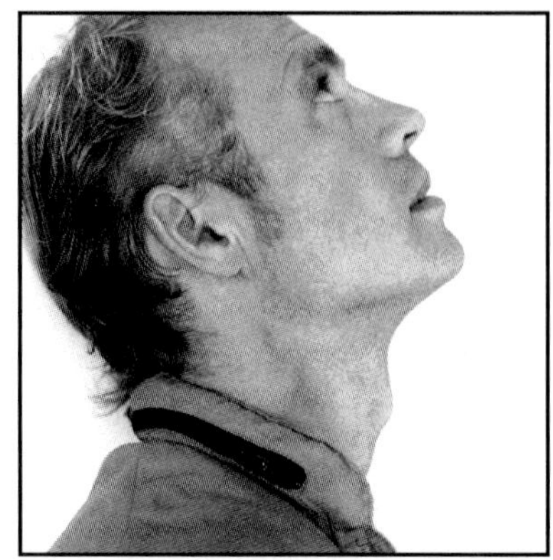
ex. 2a2 - incorrect

tion in your singing range (i.e. the lower middle) and repeat those exact notes repeating each vowel about five times. Men's starting note should be somewhere around a B flat to C (an octave below Middle C) Women's starting note should be somewhere around F to G (just below Middle C). If, in either case, these starting notes (for this or any other exercise in this program) don't work for you, experiment until you find a more comfortable place in your singing range. Keep your mouth very small and completely limp during this exercise. In this system, we are looking for *minimal mouth movement*. Excessive mouth movement invariably translates into unnecessary tension reaching well down into the throat. If it sounds like you're mumbling a little just now, don't worry about it, we'll talk about different mouth shapings and articulation techniques later on. On every other vowel ("he" and "ho") incorporate the *seven points of relaxation*, and really feel yourself going limp in this area. It is while adding these *points of relaxation* that you will most likely begin to feel "the drool" kick in. Once you can easily tap into this feeling, you will be able to do so throughout your singing session.

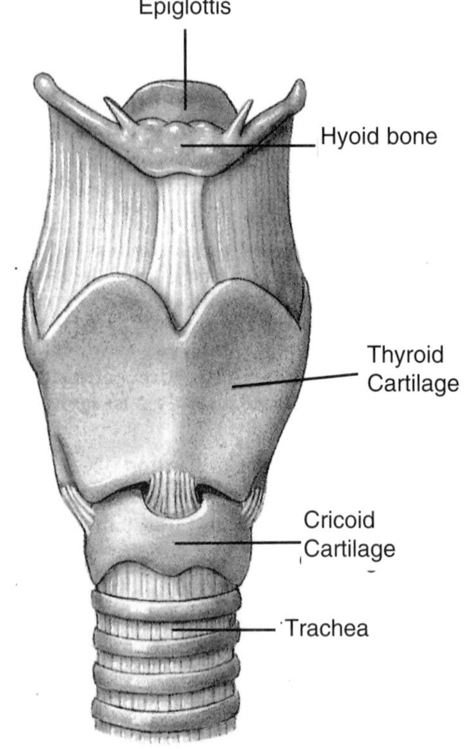

Diagram 1a

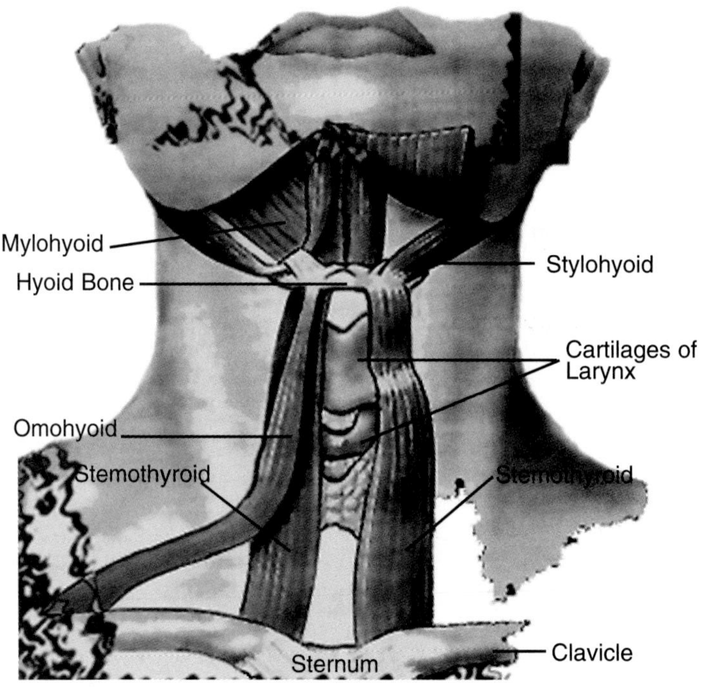

Diagram 1b

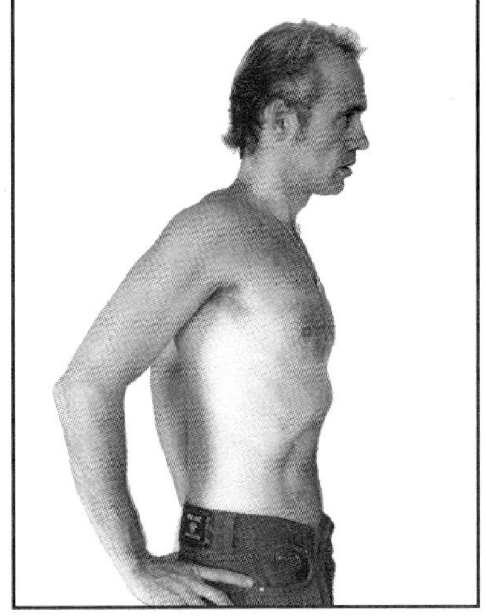
ex. 2b1 - correct

Using Ha (sounds like "hey") about 5 times
ha – ha – ha – ha – ha – ha – ha – ha – ha
Over the first 5 notes of the major scale:
do – re – mi – fa – sol – fa – mi – re – do

Then use "He" (sounds like "he/she") x about 7-10 times adding the 7 points of relaxation.
Then, on the same notes sing, "Hi" (sounds like "high") about 5 times
Then, using "Ho" (like Santa, only much quieter) about 7-10 times, adding the 7 points of relaxation.
And finally, using "Hu" (sounds like "who") about 5 times.

POSTURE

80% of posture relates directly to the support system. The better your singing posture, the better your breath control will be. This is because we are trying to create a support system that works more from reflexes than from direct manipulation of the abdominal muscles and diaphragm. The key to posture is alignment. If you align your body properly your support system will be free to work on this new high level necessary in singing. The other 20% of posture is related to the throat (open tone passage), and resonance (different cabinet sizes and shapes effect vibration characteristics).

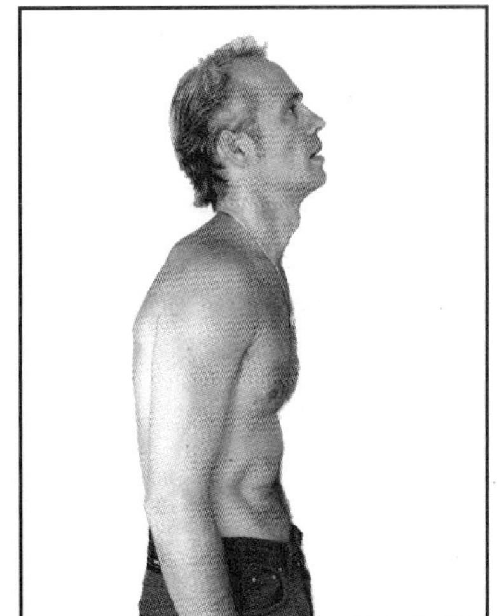
ex. 2b2 - incorrect

The Three Focal Points of Posture:

(see three step wall method for basic body posture, page 14)

1. ***Head (see ex. 2a1, 2a2):*** Tilt slightly down at a 45° to set up what we refer to as "the basic shape of the throat." This helps prevent stretching and tightening of t he muscles in the throat, freeing the overall infrastructure of the larynx.

2. ***Hips (see ex. 2b1, 2b2):*** Pulled under in a pelvic tilt to straighten back as much as possible. This is done to free up the lower and middle abdominal muscles. These are constricting/anti-constricting muscles and must be free to move out on the inhale and, in on the exhale. Do not arch the back. Arching the back tightens these muscles and severely restricts their freedom.

3. ***Rib Cage (see ex. 2c1, 2c2):*** An "open rib cage technique" is used in *The Art of Body Singing*. If you study the mechanics of breathing in a book on anatomy, you will generally find a description of what's called "costal breathing." This basically means that the rib cage expands during inhalation and collapses during exhalation. This is fine for everyday use, but in singing, far more control and endurance are required than can be achieved by "costal breathing." An "open rib cage technique" is maintained by using the external intercostal muscles

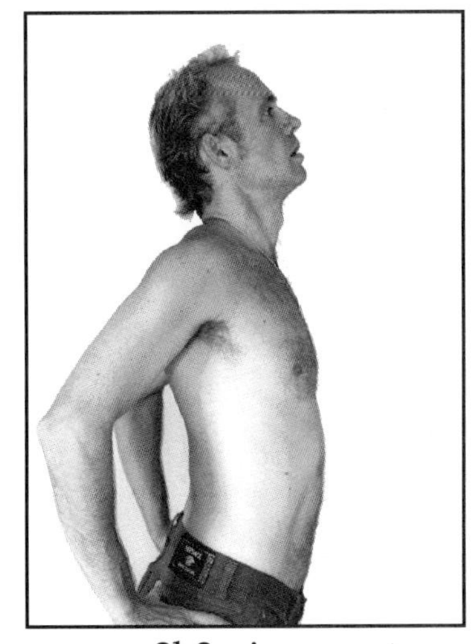
ex. 2b3 - incorrect

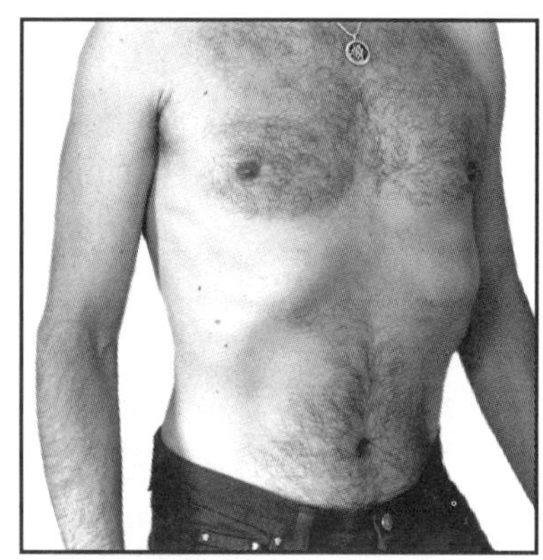
ex. 2c1 - correct

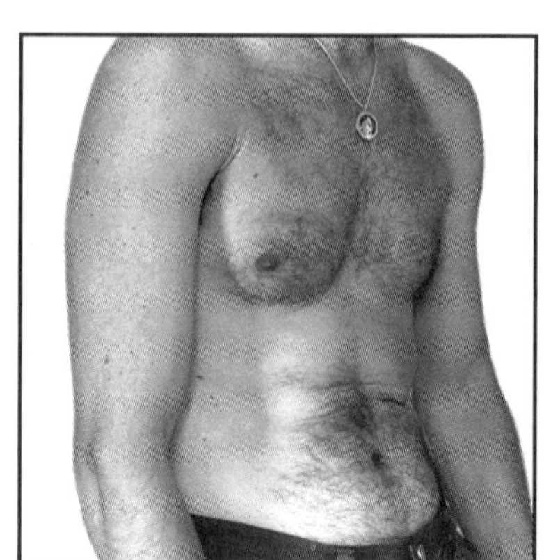
ex. 2c2 - incorrect

(the outside group of muscles located in between the ribs) to raise the ribs and expand the chest (see diagram #2 on page 16). If the "open rib cage technique" is maintained during singing, then you are no longer relying on the the rib muscles for exhalation, but instead upon the much more powerful and controllable diaphragm and abdominal muscles below your lungs.

It must be noted here that many systems teach diaphragmatic breathing in a collapsed chest posture. It is my belief that for less demanding singing this can certainly be adequate. However, it is also my belief that for more demanding singing, this is highly inadequate. The problem is that you will begin to push and shove with your diaphragm and abdominal muscles. This is often the cause behind many vocal health problems, a result of over-pressurizing the vocal cords. Pushing with the support system also tends to produce a very harsh and undesirable sounding tone. Even if you are trying to achieve a very grindy, aggressive tone, pushing is not how you'll achieve it. The big advantage to the "open rib cage technique" is freedom. This technique frees up the diaphragm and upper abdominal muscles so that they may be used more upon reflexes than by conscious manipulation. That benefit alone can dramatically influence a more relaxed delivery in a singer. So, spend some time developing this posture. What feels awkward at first will soon become so natural that anything less will be obviously inferior.

Three Step Wall Method for Attaining Posture:

Stance 1

1. ***Sitting against the wall (see ex 3a).*** Stand with your back against the wall, with your shoulders down and relaxed, and your hips in a pelvic tilt position (tilt your pelvis forward as if you are trying to relocate your tailbone directly under your belly button, while keeping your shoulders back), keeping your knees as bent as necessary to feel your entire back touching the wall (almost a sitting position). Tilt head down to a 45°. Slowly walk your feet under your body until your heels are touching the wall. Keep your knees slightly bent to maintain a straight back.

2. ***Step out over front foot (see ex. 3b).*** Step away from the wall over your front dominant foot (if you're right handed that's probably your right foot) placing seventy percent of your weight over that front foot. Think of a line running under the toe of

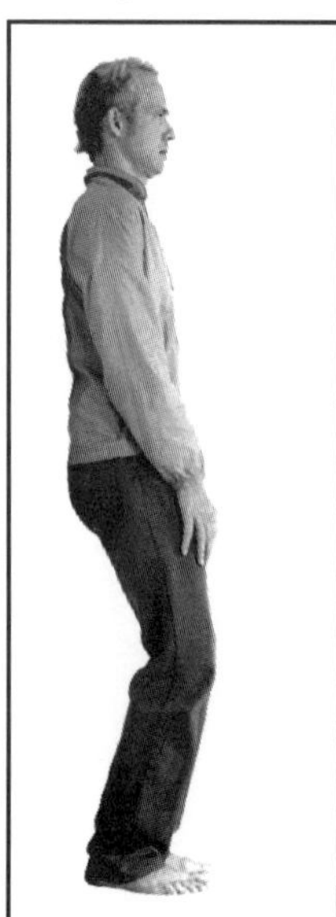
ex. 3a

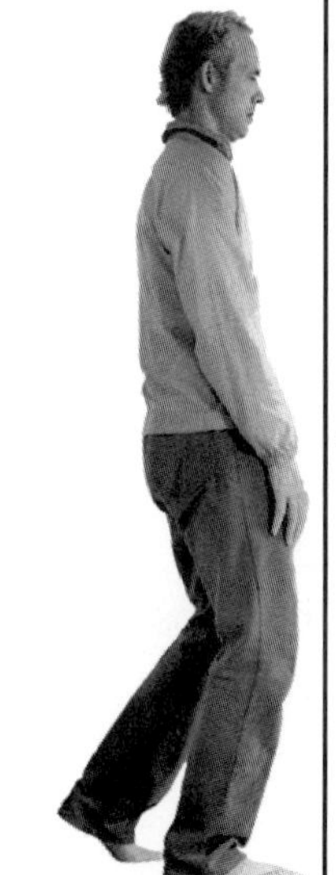
ex. 3b

ex. 3c

your back foot. The heel of your front foot should now be on that same line (in other words, don't step out too deep). Your feet should be about shoulder width apart. Come up on the ball of the back foot leaving thirty percent of your weight over that foot. In fact, think of most of your weight being placed on the balls of both of your feet. Be sure not to lose any of the alignment achieved in step 1. When necessary you should be able to shift weight easily from front to back feet without losing your body alignment. This comes in very handy when singing and playing an instrument simultaneously.

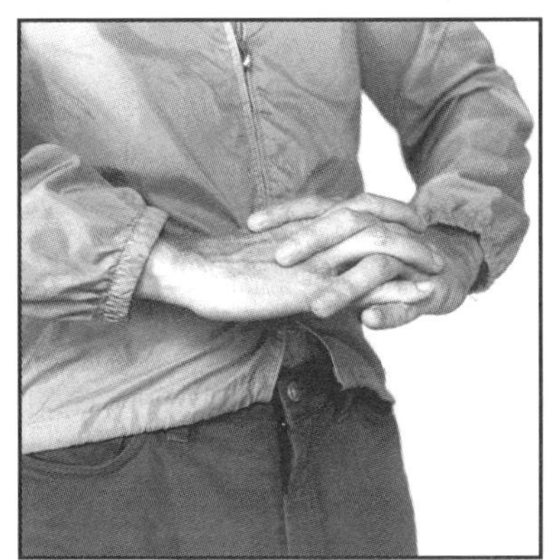

ex. 4a

3. *Lift into open rib cage position (see ex. 3c, also diagram 2).* Imagine a cable attached to your chest. As you take a deep breath way down into your body, while opening your rib cage with your intercostal muscles (not your back muscles), that cable is going to lift your torso up about an inch and keep it there. In other words, if you were wearing a long robe that touched the floor this step in posture would lift that robe off the floor by about one to one and one half inches, and keep it raised from breath to breath. Be careful to acknowledge that this is the torso lifting the robe and not the shoulders. Keep your shoulders down and relaxed. Do not allow your chest to collapse during singing or between breaths. If you do collapse, you will not realize the full range motion of the support system, and this will severely limit the endurance and control of your breath in singing. After some practice, you should be able to lift your chest and expand your upper rib cage without the aid of taking a breath. When you can do this, you will have truly discovered the independence of the intercostal muscles.

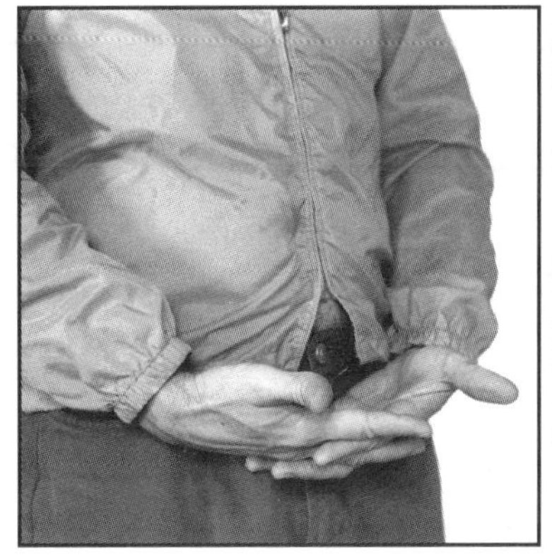

ex. 4b

Practice these steps until you can easily just step into posture from a standing position. Really teaching your body to maintain these alignments will take some weeks of practice. It will feel rather wooden at first, but I assure you that it will become very natural and supple with time.

THE KICK START TECHNIQUE

This technique is to be used with the following exercise:

1. *Thumbs on navel as measuring guide (see ex. 4A).* Lace fingers together with palms facing body. Place thumbs on naval (as a measuring guide) and cup lower edge of hands down under your belt line to the lower abdominal muscles. At this point palms should be facing upward.

2. *Cupped hands on lower abs (see ex. 4b).* Gently lift (never push) lower abdominals while practicing the *The Way Down Exercise.* This is to help locate and stimulate these lower deeper muscles.

THE WAY DOWN EXERCISE

There are a few objectives with this exercise. The title, *The Way Down Exercise,* means that you are singing *way down* in your range (very low notes), and that you are focusing *way down* in your support system (the lower abdominal muscles). The other objective with this exercise is to focus on maintaining your high chest and open rib cage position.

Some systems only develop the upper abdominal muscles and the diaphragm for breath support. Be aware that the closer the muscles are to the lungs, the higher the possibility of forcing air, which inevitably leads to oversinging and strain. This is invariably the case when singing the lower range. This is due to the fact that pitch is created by the speed at which the vocal cords vibrate. The higher the pitch, the faster the speed of vibration. The lower the pitch, the slower the speed of vibration. These vibrations are directly affected by the amount of air used during phonation (creating sound with voice). Therefore, working out in your lower range is a great place to get acquainted with the lower support system. These lower abdominals are farther away from the lungs and make for wonderful fine tuning support system muscles. Also, don't forget that even though you're stimulating these lower abs with the *kick start technique,* you don't want to develop any habits of squeezing or over firming anywhere in your support system. You are not looking for rock hard firmness, but instead a more supple firmness that can shift support from lower to upper abdominals and diaphragm very quickly and easily.

Pay close attention to how this exercise sounds on the Volume One recording. Remember not to gargle the tone as you go lower in your range,

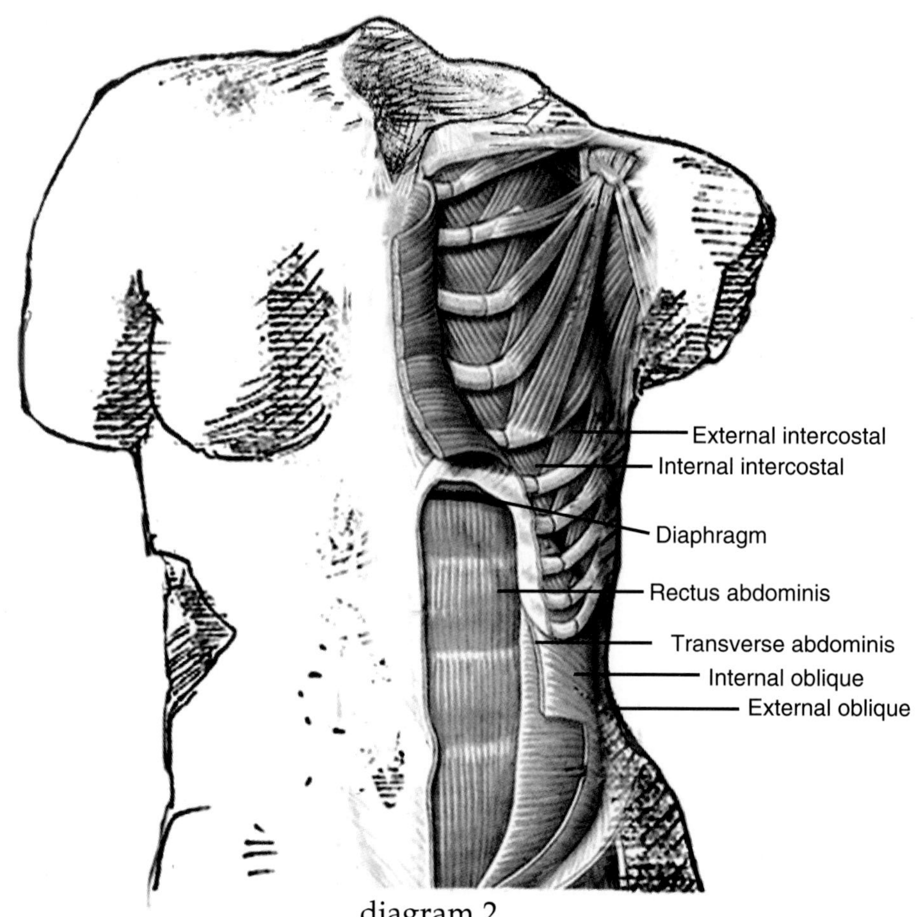

diagram 2

but instead to *release* the tone. As you get lower and lower (all the way down to the *no note district*), the size of the tone should diminish until it is completely inaudible. This is to help you teach yourself not to let the tone be manipulated by the constricting muscles in the throat. In many ways this exercise should be an extension of the *Drool Exercise*, the end result being a warmed up and relaxed throat.

Listen now to example on **Volume One** recording.

Standing in your new, great singing posture, watch yourself in a mirror as you practice the exercise (a mirror will save you a lot of time in really learning to sing in posture). Your objective is to sing the exercise in its entirety without allowing your posture to deteriorate. The first thing to watch for is your ribs collapsing and your chest sinking. It is difficult at first to differentiate the intercostal muscles used to maintain the open rib cage position from the air in the lungs. It is very tempting at first to resort back to the much easier costal breathing (meaning that the rib cage and chest expand with inhalation and collapse with exhalation). It takes some practice, but it is important that you teach yourself to maintain the big open posture. Don't worry if the lower ribs shrink with exhalation. It is the upper ribs and chest that concern us most. Also, watch in the mirror that your head does not start rising up and that you do not begin arching your back.

The *Way Down Exercise* is done on repeated pitches using the musical consonant "m" with five vowels creating a *continuous energy* non-breaking tone. That means you hum the "m" between the vowels "e" (see), "a" (rhymes with say),"i" (try), "o" (go) and "u" (true) while singing the same pitch five times on one breath without stopping the tone.

Me, Ma, Mi, Mo, Mu

Use nice, relaxed, slightly airy (without pushing) medium-sized tone. Start in your lower middle range (men start around D below Middle C and women start around G below Middle C). Sing through all of the vowels sustaining the last one ("u") until you are nearly out of breath. Then move the vowel down one half step. Stop singing, but maintain the big open posture. Take a huge breath, through your nose and down into your lower abdominals, then start the series over on the new lower note. This is known as "moving the exercise." If you don't have an instrument handy, just start in a comfortable place in your range. Ultimately, you need to learn to do these exercises completely out of your head anyway. So, once you've memorized the exercise, start practicing without a reference note from an instrument. This is necessary to teach you self-sufficiency, as ultimately the voice is a free-standing instrument.

SPEAKING THE MELODY

It is very important that a singer understands the connection between singing and speaking. Any melody that can be sung can also be spoken. The biggest departure from speaking to singing is in the rhythm. With singing, we begin to sustain the vowels that in speaking, we cut short. Though they are generally located in a narrow part of the vocal range, if you listen closely to most speaking voices you will hear plenty of melodies. This is, in fact, the premise to most contemporary systems of voice "if you can speak, you can sing." While there is certainly a lot of truth in that statement, it is my view that singing and speaking are first cousins, not twins. The singers that wish to elevate themselves to *high-level singing* must assemble a far superior instrument (voice) to the singer satisfied with the thin "speak-singing" voice so prevalent in today's contemporary music.

That said, the advantages to first learning this exercise of *Speaking the Melody* must not be overlooked. Those advantages include comfort, coordination, and naturalization. Singing is "connecting the dots" and is truly a democracy of its four components (1. Inner Ear, 2. Throat, 3. Support System, 4. Resonance). The easiest way to achieve this coordination is by concentrating largely on comfort. Keep things light at this stage in your development. In fact, I call this period of a singers growth *The Ease*, because I want their singing to have a nice easy quality to it. It is far too common in contemporary singing systems to have singers shouting at the beginning of their development. These "shouting" techniques are usually taught in the guise of "support system development" and "voice opening techniques." I disagree with this approach. I feel it can only teach singers the bad habits of pushing and straining from the beginning of their study. It is far more constructive to teach singers comfort, control and coordination from the get-go. This will make graduating into more ambitious singing a realistic transition.

It is often during *the ease* period that I will suggest a singer spend some time with some old jazz standard ballads. These tunes are conducive to a lighter touch. Ballads in general are great for developing breath support and, in my opinion, the older jazz is a sophisticated, yet straight forward style of music that can do nothing but wonderful things for a singer's ear. I must certainly pay tribute to a former teacher of mine, Steve Heck, for enlightening me to the virtue of singing Jazz Standards.

Also, by *Speaking the Melody* you can listen at this very formative time for that certain *singy* quality singers tend to get. This is a good time to think about being very dry and style-less in your singing. This will make way for a very natural, personal and honest delivery with your music. If you are practicing this technique with music other than your own, really try to hear your own speaking voice come through. It is my view that imitation in vocal technique training can be more of a hindrance than a help, especially at the beginning. For one, it takes a singer a long time to accurately register what they're hearing when they produce sound with their voice. Anyone who's recorded themselves and listened back to the results can attest to this reality. This is due to the vibrations occurring inside your head during phonation in conjunction with the sound exiting your mouth. It's a strange mixture. Therefore, if you are hearing something from the receiving end, and trying to reproduce it from the giving end, your challenge is obvious.

Some singers, though with some diligence, tend to master the art of imitating a few of their heroes. The problem with this approach is that their personal interpretation skills are limited to something akin to muscle memory singing. Regardless of the mood of the piece, their techniques are limited to what they learned through imitation and always sound the same. So do yourself a favor, and start naturalizing your voice through this wonderful exercise of *Speaking the Melody.*

Listen now to example on **Volume One** recording.

After warming up with the exercises you know so far, choose one or two songs with which you are already fairly familiar. If you can't think of one, try a children's song or perhaps a Christmas song that you already know and enjoy. Sing through a section of the song (a verse or chorus, etc...) a few times in a very comfortable voice. Begin hearing yourself curtail the lengths of the vowels in the song more and more until you are literally *Speaking the Melody.* If, at any point, you're having difficulty, lower the melody in pitch. It's important to understand the exercise, and then gradually make the difficulty level higher.

THE 3 AIR RATIOS

Air passing through the vocal cords, causing them to vibrate produces the initial pitch and tone for voice production. We then turn those initial vibrations into bigger tones with "resonance" from our body (discussed at length later in the program). Therefore, we can conclude that resonance plus air equals tone. Knowing this allows us to understand that there is always air under the tone. *The 3 Air Ratios* helps us to identify the air on top of the tone (sometimes referred to as "free air.")

1. Number One Ratio or Fully Supported Tone (see diagram # 3): On this *ratio* the air is completely underneath the tone. This is the most efficient tone you will produce. This is the tone heard from most healthy speaking voices, because it is the most projecting tone for the least amount of energy used.

As an advanced singer, this is the biggest (meaning loudest and most resonant) tone you will ever produce, because all of the air used is being turned into resonance. You will also find that as you sing higher and higher in your range this will be the hardest *ratio* to maintain. This difficulty is due to unnecessary muscle constriction in the throat and very often from excess pushing from the support system, both contributing to an excessive level of *throat pressure* (covered later under this subject). So, for now, stay with *the ease* and gain the coordination to take this *ratio* to the top of your singing range.

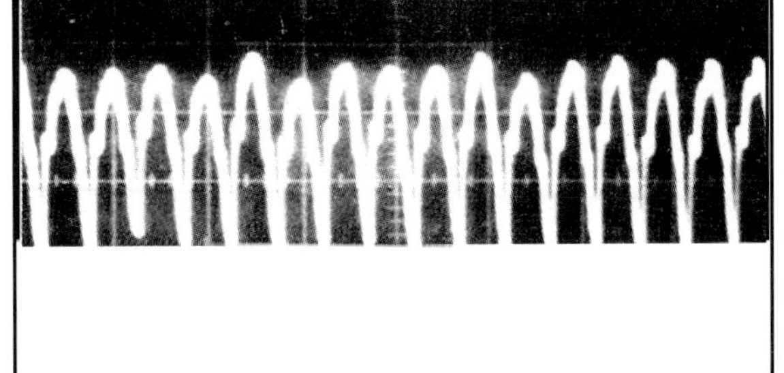

Diagram 3 - Number 1 Ratio

2. ***Number Two Ratio or Full Tone with Air (see diagram 4):*** This is still a sizable tone, but with a very audible bite taken out of it. Using the same amount of energy used for a *number one ratio*, this tone will be lighter and have a wet airy quality to it (see *buffer air* below). As you sing higher in your range this tone should be easier at first to execute than the *number one ratio* tone. This once again is due to the subject of *throat pressure* (covered later in this subject).

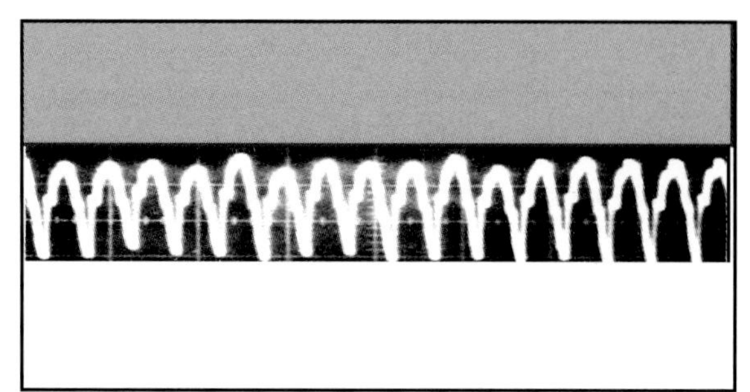

Diagram 4 - Number 2 Ratio

3. ***Number Three Ratio or Air Note (see diagram 5):*** Picture Marilyn Monroe singing "Happy Birthday, Mr. President." This is the lightest tone you will articulate and still be audible. This is a very wet and airy tone, but it is important to be aware of not creating excess air while singing the *number three ratio*. Remember, this is the same amount of energy used for the *number one ratio* , but with a significant *release* in the throat (see *buffer air* and *throat pressure* below).

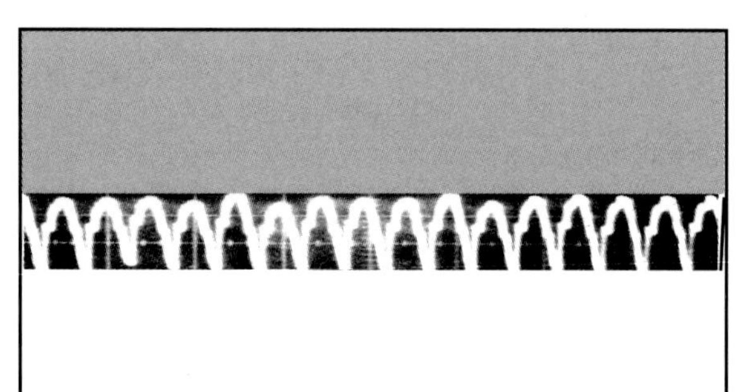

Diagram 5 – Number 3 Ratio

Listen now to example on **Volume One** recording...

1. Counting one through ten on the same pitch in a comfortable place in your range, switch from the *number one ratio* to the *number two ratio* and finally to the *number three ratio*. You should hear a very audible decrease in the volume of the more airy tones. Remember not to increase air as you're using *buffer air* here (see below). Start moving the pitch around in your range to fully experience the different *ratios*.

2. Now, begin sustaining the ratios. Starting in a comfortable place in your range using the word "hey," sustain the long "a" vowel, staying loyal to the ratio on which you began. Then, move on to the other two ratios and repeat. Once this is comfortable, move the pitch around in your range to fully experience sustaining the ratios. Remember to use your ear as your guide here. It is very common to start out on a *number one ratio* and slip to a *number two ratio*. Remember to *listen* for this and then *feel* the feeling involved in maintaining the ratio or adjusting back to the original ratio if you've slipped out. "Adjusting on the fly" is of primary importance in the performance world. Constantly recognizing that the ear is the first part of the voice will save you from the trap that many singers fall into of *auto-pilot singing*.

3. Now begin singing with the *three air ratios*: First, experiment with a short section of a song that you are familiar with (a verse or chorus, etc...). Start out singing the entire section on a *number three ratio* which should be the easiest of all (see *throat pressure*). Then, repeat the same section on a *number two ratio*, then finally a *number one ratio*. If the song is a little high in your range, you might experience some trouble with the *number one ratio* (see *throat pressure*). So, for now, sing the song lower in your range. Once this becomes comfortable, start practicing the ratios by staying loyal to one at a time for entire songs. This is not about interpretation just yet, this is about technique. The way to really learn a technique is by exaggeration. So, have fun with this.

TOOL SONGS

Now's a good time to pick out a couple of songs from your collection over which to practice your techniques. Keep it down to two or three songs for now. Sing these songs either along with a recording or A Capella. If you can play an instrument while singing, do so after you've had a good vocal workout. This way you can fully concentrate on the task at hand. Structuring a good singing session will be discussed later in this program.

THROAT PRESSURE

Throat pressure in singing is a very tricky subject. Especially since one of the first things we learn in proper vocalization is how to relax the constrictor muscles in our throat, so as not to over-pressurize our vocal cords. This makes the term *throat pressure* sound a bit contradictory.

Air passes through the trachea (windpipe) during the breathing process. During phonation, air stimulates the vocal cords (which are housed in the trachea inside the larynx) causing them to vibrate, creating the initial pitch and tone. (See diagrams 6, 7, & 8). Because this miracle of voice production is so automatic to most humans, the initiation of the vocal cords is basically an involuntary one. Muscles and a pair of pivoting cartilages (the arytenoid cartilages) in the larynx are employed (largely by the nervous system) to bring the cords to their close, yet slightly apart position for proper vibration (see diagram 7 and 8). When the cords are properly aligned during phonation, one should experience (when concentrating) a mild sensation inside the throat. There should be absolutely no discomfort.

This sensation should be thought of as *conversation level throat pressure*. The reason for the term *throat pressure,* is that when the vocal cords come together there is a slight pressure created between the cords and the air in the lungs. It is this slight pressure that creates the initial vibration in the cords that can then be amplified by additional vibration throughout the body ("resonance" will be covered at length later in this program). This slight *conversation level throat pressure* is both necessary and healthy. What's unhealthy is any additional *throat pressure* caused by constriction in the throat or pushing too much air *through the throat* from the support system. Therefore, you must learn to take the journey inward, inside the throat and *feel* for that perfect level of *throat pressure*. Not only will it mean everything to your vocal health to master this feeling, but also to your tone quality (more about that later).

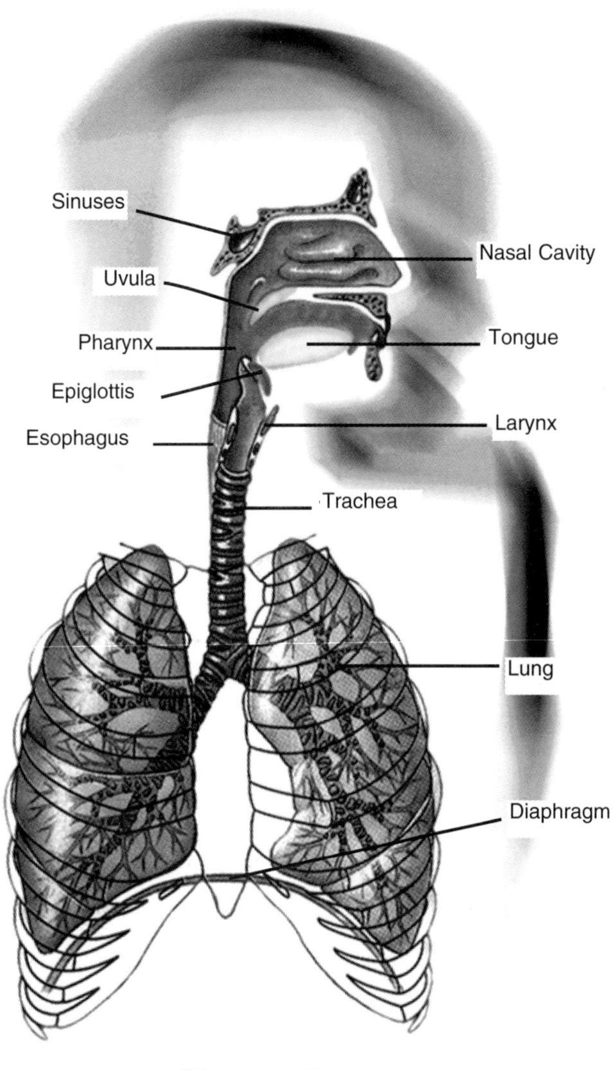

Diagram 6

BUFFER AIR

I like to illustrate *buffer air* in relation to the *Three Air Ratios*. If there were a *ratio four*, it would be zero *throat pressure*, It would also be zero vibration of the cords and therefore zero tone. It would basically be air passing through the trachea and vocal cords without producing any vibration. Remember, without a slight pressure between the cords and the air in the lungs there can be no vibration of the cords. At *number three ratio*, the cords move closer together and we begin to pressurize a bit of air, resulting in cord vibration and the beginning of tone. At a *number two ratio*, the

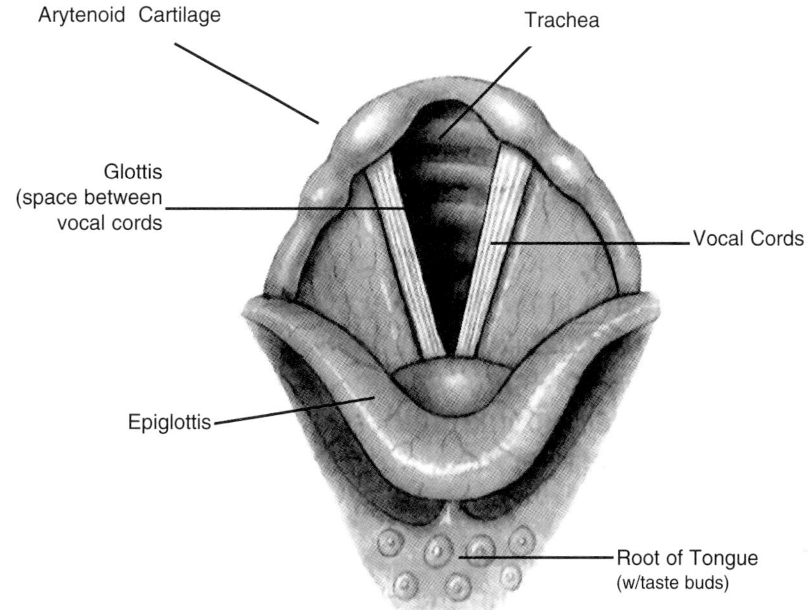

open position
Diagram 7

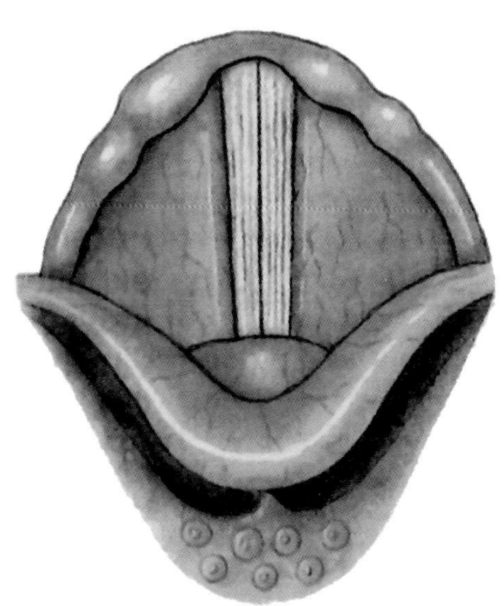

closed position
Diagram 8

cords move even closer together and we pressurize a bit more still, resulting in a very noticeable increase in tone color and volume using the same exact amount of energy and air. And finally, at a *number one ratio,* the cords come as close as they can for healthy singing, resulting in what's referred to as a "fully supported tone."

With over-pressurization, the cords begin to touch (somewhat violently), causing irritations leading to vocal disorders. There should be no audible air on top of the *number one ratio*. And, for the same amount of energy used for the airier *ratios,* this should be the loudest and fullest tone of all. As stated earlier, the higher in your range that you sing, the more likely you are to over-pressurize the *number one ratio*. This is because it requires more air for the vocal cords to vibrate at a faster speed to create the higher pitch. This makes maintaining *conversation level throat pressure* in the upper range difficult. It simply requires some methodical and patient practice, as well as some great techniques which we'll learn later on in the system. So for now, stay with *the ease* and just master the different techniques you've been learning thus far. We'll get to the tough stuff soon enough.

GUSHING

Listen to example on **Volume One** recording.

Gushing is a random release of air during phonation. It is usually a result of pushing with the support system. Check your posture and back off! We are currently observing a *No Black Sheep Rule* in our practice sessions. This implies that we are *listening* to ourselves and making corrections where they need to be made. If you maintain *buffer air*, *gushing* will not be possible.

THE TONGUE ROLL AND LIP ROLL

ex. 5a

These two exercises are very popular in contemporary singing systems, and there is good reason for this. When done correctly, they are wonderful mechanics exercises. They help coordinate the *four parts of the voice* beautifully.
The Tongue Roll is executed like a spanish "r." The tip of the tongue vibrates against the hard corner of the gum ridge, behind the top front teeth and the sharp rising arc of the hard pallet, while creating a tone with the vocal cords. If you are not getting a tone with the vibration of the tongue, you will be creating what some diction systems call an unvoiced consonant (a consonant produced without the aid of the vocal cords). In this instance, the consonant will be a "t" sound as in "time." Think more along the lines a vibrating "tr," as in "truck," or, for a softer entry into the exercise, try "dr" as in drive. At first, just practice short and gentle entries with this exercise. Once you get the hang of it move on to the extended exercises listed below.

"The Lip Roll" is executed by puckering your lips forward with your thumb and index finger placed in the dimple area of the cheeks, pushing slightly out and slightly up to create loose and relaxed lips (see ex 5a). Roll the lips (sometimes called "bubbles," "raspberries," "car revving," etc...), while creating a tone with the vocal cords. If you are vibrating your lips, but not initiating a tone, you are probably concentrating on the consonant "p" (you can produce "p" without creating tone from the vocal cords). Instead, concentrate on the consonant "b" with your entries into the Lip Roll, as this should help facilitate the tone.

Here are the rules for the mechanics of both the Tongue Roll and the Lip Roll. In both exercises, concentrate on how slow and relaxed you can make the vibration of the tongue or the lips. If either are vibrating in a fast, spasmodic sort of way, you are "over-singing." This means that you are singing *through your throat* instead of *behind your throat*. Something you will hear a lot in *The Art of Body Singing* is to sing *backwards into the body*. Ultimately, this means you are going *inside your body* where everything happens in singing, and you are coordinating the process from its source. Everything in singing is connected to the series of physical feelings that make sound from the voice possible. If you are "over-singing," you are basically "pushing" air out of your lungs *through your throat* and singing from the throat up. This can result in a very unhealthy voice and, ultimately, bad tone.

Concentrate on a *number one ratio* for both the Tongue Roll and the Lip Roll. One of the most tangible assets of these two exercises is that much of the *throat pressure* needed for phonation is transferred from the throat to the lips or tongue (depending, of course, on which exercise you are practicing). You will clearly feel this with one of the up-coming exercises (TR mm ah and LR mm ah exercises). This makes practicing with the *number one ratio* very safe and practical at this time. Remember, the ear is the first part of the voice. If you're hearing air on top of the tone with these exercises, your not in a *number one ratio*. If you're having difficulty executing these exercises on the *number one ratio* practice altering from a tone on that *ratio* into the Tongue Roll or the Lip Roll exercises. Most students have an easier time with one or the other of these exercises. Some students, no matter how hard they try, can only execute one of the two exercises. And a small percentage of students cannot execute either of the exercises. It has been my experience that with practice most students can achieve great results with both exercises. If one is more difficult than the other, do not give up on it. Even though they appear very similar just now, they are different enough exercises that the ideal is to possess both. Thoroughly examining your mechanical difficulties in singing, and then overcoming them, will teach you far more than the techniques that come to you without any struggle.

If you think back in the program you might notice that the Drool Exercise was done basically on a *number three ratio*, the *Way Down Exercise* was done basically on a *number two ratio*, and now the Tongue Roll and Lip Roll should be done on a *number one ratio*. This structure is designed to enhance your sensibilities and ear to the *mechanical switch* requirements necessary in producing the different *air ratios*. This is also partly do to the practical process of warming up. With *buffer air*, the lighter the *ratio* (i.e. *number three ratio* being lightest), the easier on the throat. This is due to throat pressure. So, regardless of one's ability, always start with the lightest and progress to the more difficult.

Listen now to example on **Volume One** recording.

Start with a sustained Tongue Roll. Using a mirror to monitor excellent posture and the second hand of a clock to monitor progress, sustain a nice easy *number one ratio* Tongue Roll for as long as possible. Then move one half step in either direction and explore this exercise throughout your range. Keep it nice and comfortable. It will be more comfortable to use the airier ratios for the higher part of your range. That's ok for starters, but keep teaching yourself what it *feels* and *sounds* like as you keep shaving off the air. When it gets too high or low, reverse direction and work on coordination. If you're having trouble sustaining this exercise, really work on your entries. After your entries begin to smooth out (for many this is only after several tries) begin to draw them out to a more sustained Tongue Roll.

Men start around a D and women start around a G below Middle C. If these starting notes aren't comfortable, experiment until you find what suits you. Sustain the Tongue Roll as long as possible, then move the note one half step up or down, just before your air supply is completely exhausted. Repeat the exercise on a new note.

Repeat the exact procedure listed above with Lip Roll exercise.

THE "TONGUE ROLL MM AH" EXERCISE

This is a coordination exercise designed to get you from the ideal set-up of the Tongue Roll (or Lip Roll) exercise, to the nicely contained world of a healthy hum, to the more precarious world of creating a tone.

Listen to example on **Volume One** recording.

Note that the first examples on the recording are done on a *number two ratio* for ease and then changed to a *number one ratio*. Even though we are attempting to do the Tongue Roll and Lip Roll exercises on a *number one ratio,* our first concern is always comfort.

Without stopping the flow of tone, energy, or air, move seamlessly from a comfortable Tongue Roll to a comfortable hum on an "m," to a comfortable tone on "ah" (as is "ball"). Remember the *no black sheep rule*, and listen not to allow any changes from one part of the exercise to the next (i.e. differences in volume, pitch, or *air ratios*). Once the exercise becomes comfortable, it should be executed on the *number one ratio.*

Men start around a D and women around a G below Middle C. Move the exercise just before breath is completely exhausted and repeat exercise on new note.

Sustain the final tone in the exercise as long as possible. *Listen* and *feel* what this tone sounds and feels like. It should still be a *number one ratio*, and it should feel comfortable and sound clear. If you are hearing any *throat rattle* or *throat distortion* (see following explanation) being added to the tone you are pushing, so back off.

Repeat the above procedure for the *Lip Roll Mm Ah* exercise.

THROAT RATTLE OR THROAT DISTORTION

Throat rattle or throat distortion are caused by singing *through the throat* and rattling the phlegm and mucous that is generally present to one degree or another in all of our throats. In *The Art of Body Singing,* our goal is to sing *behind the throat* or *over the throat* and never *through the throat.* This is a strange concept for many at first, because it seems to create a contradiction in anatomy. This is ultimately about singing with the perfect *throat pressure*, and letting the other elements of the voice (i.e. resonance, ratios, etc,) create the size, color and projection you are after. *Throat Rattle* is an obvious sign of over-pressurizing in the throat, via constriction or pushing. So, correct this problem while we're still working on *the ease* level of energy.

You must constantly remember that singing is *connecting the dots*. Only so much can be expected from the throat, or from the support system, or from resonance. Any over-reliance on these individual parts will result in an obvious imbalance. Therefore, the answer is always in the correct distribution of responsibility between the components of the voice. Think of it as a true democracy. The end result of the *four parts of the voice* working in harmony together is so much greater than that of the voice where the power is in an obvious imbalance.

TONGUE ROLL 1-5 EXERCISE AND THE LIP ROLL 1-5 EXERCISE

This helps develop the *air spigot* in your support system for singing. The *air spigot* is the imagery I use for the control of the support system. Air requirements are different as pitches vary. Use your ear as your guide in this exercise. If you're getting louder as you ascend in pitch, you are *overcompensating* the *air spigot* with too much air. If you are getting quieter as you sing lower, you are *undercompensating* the *air spigot* with too little air. Also, pay close attention that you don't change your *air ratio* as you move the pitch. This happens most commonly while ascending in pitch. This relates back to the issue of *throat pressure*. Your job here is to relax your throat and not allow your support system to push (the better the posture, the less likelihood of pushing). This is about management. Don't race through the exercise. Loop each series of notes several times until you're comfortable enough to move on. If your tone is getting bright (as in a falsetto kind of tone) as you enter into your upper range, that is just fine for now. Just keep it light and relaxed. We will deal with the subjects of tone quality and resonance at great lengths in the subsequent volumes.

Listen now to the example on **Volume One** recording.

Using the first five notes of the major scale, move the exercises up and down to develop the coordination necessary in moving a tone.

These are the same notes we used for the Drool Exercise, only now sustain the last note for a short time and then move the note one half step in whatever direction you are moving. Men start around a B or C one octave below Middle C and women start around a G below Middle C. Begin by moving the exercise upward (ascending) until it becomes too difficult, then begin looping one series of 1-5 at a time until it feels comfortable to move on. Once you've passed your comfort level, begin moving the exercise back down towards your lower range.

TONGUE ROLLING AND LIP ROLLING OVER MELODIES

Once you've reached a certain comfort level with these exercises, Tongue Rolling and Lip Rolling over melodies is a great way to find a real fluidity in practicing them. This exercise also makes for a great warm up to do in the car. I'm not a big fan of car singing. I've seen too many strained voices as a result, but with a little understanding, there are certain things which can be practiced in the car. Of course, it is never advisable to do anything which might distract your driving, so always use discretion.

Listen now to example on **Volume One** recording.

Start with a few comfortable melodies that you already know. If you can't think of one, try a children's song or Christmas carol. Basically practice the Tongue Roll and the Lip Roll over these melodies. Stay light. Once it feels comfortable, start shaving off the air and moving closer and closer to a *number one ratio* for the entire melody. Once you've gone through your earlier warm ups, this is something that you can be doing throughout the day. This is a great coordination development exercise. Have fun!

SINGING AN OCTAVE BELOW THE MELODY

It is very common for singers to sing poorly in their lower range. This is mostly do to a lack of training in singing in their lower range. Most singers are so attracted to the acrobatic upper middle and upper range, that the lower range is often ignored. This seems a shame since singing is ultimately acting, and the emotions portrayed in the lower range can be strikingly different from the emotions portrayed in the upper range. Therefore, full range singing generally translates into a full range emotional performance. So kill multiple birds with one stone. Sing your lower range for relaxation, for comfort and safety in car singing, and for full range singing practice.

Listen now to example on **Volume One** recording.

Once you've warmed up, put on a recording of a song with which you are already familiar. Now gently sing along with that song on the proper melody. Once the melody is firmly in your ear, begin singing the same melody exactly one octave lower. This should be in a very relaxed and released tone much like that of the *Way Down Exercise*. This should not only be relaxing for your throat, but should prove to be a great workout for your lower range as well as for your ear. This is both a great relaxation exercise and a safe solution to car singing.

SILENT SINGING

Silent Singing is of course just that, singing completely in your head without uttering a sound. Silent Singing is a great exercise for your ear and your body. The first goal is to be able to sing silently and really monitor that no tension is building in your throat or anywhere else in your body. So be completely limp. Next try adding some of the physical mechanics (i.e. posture, air ratios, etc.) that you are currently learning (we will be adding many more mechanics in subsequent volumes). This is a good way to practice *feeling* inside your body at any given time or place. Try Silent Singing first with a song you know well, then add it to your list of safe car singing techniques (of course, never losing sight of the concentration necessary for driving).

YOUR VOLUME ONE WORK OUT AND WARM UP ROUTINE

Singing is a physical proposition. Warm Up! As we stated earlier in the program it might be easier for you to compile all of the exercise examples from the Volume One recording onto one tape. Do this in the order in which they appear in the program. Use that compilation tape to really grasp all there is to grasp from each exercise, and to memorize each exercise. Then begin practicing your routine completely from memory.

At this point use what we've learned in Volume One in the following order.

1. Drool Exercise with the Seven Points of Relaxation (2 minutes)
2. Way Down Exercise (2 minutes)
3. Timed Sustained Tongue Roll Exercise (2 minutes)
4. Tongue Roll Mm Ahh Exercise (2 minutes)
5. Tongue Roll 1-5 Exercise (2 minutes)
6. Timed Sustained Lip Roll Exercise (2 minute)
7. Lip Roll Mm Ahh Exercise (2 minutes)
8. Lip Roll 1-5 Exercise (2 minutes)
9. Light to Medium Sustained Tones Practicing Three Air Ratios (2 minutes)
10. Gently Speaking the Melody on Number One Ratio (2 minutes)

So far, that's just a well-organized twenty minute workout routine.

Now, practice singing using your *tool songs*. Start out very gently on a *number two ratio,* and feel how good it feels to be warmed up. Gently make the transition to the *number one ratio* without changing your energy. The size of the tone will automatically grow with this transition. Once you've stayed loyal to the *number one ratio*, begin deliberately varying the *ratios*. Absorb the differences in size, color and physical demands of the *three air ratios*.

Now, sing any other material you might be working on for as long as you have time. If that's only ten minutes, then so be it. But if it's longer, great. Stay relaxed, keep checking in with the mirror, keep using your hands to massage the *seven points of relaxation* (as tension can creep in at any time) and keep *listening* to yourself. Have a lot of fun and join us for Volumes 2–4 of *The Art of Body Singing*.

Best Wishes,

Please visit Bodysinging.com to purchase easy to follow routine CDs of the exercises contained in this book.

NOTES FROM THE AUTHOR

BRECK ALAN'S DELUXE TRIO
The Soiled Dove
(1949 Market St./LODO, Denver)Thursday March 2
10 — 11:15 (Victor Towle opens, then Breck Alan charms
your pants off, then John Mckay goes on 11:30ish
(303-299-0100)

BRECK ALAN
with "SIDESHOW MIKE"
THE SMOKIN' UPRIGHT BASS MAN
POWER VOICE AND ACOUSTIC GUITAR!
come get your 50¢ mystery can
WEDNESDAY NIGHTS
@ NICK'S ON THE HILL
its a grooving happyfest
(BOULDER, 1143 13TH ST., 440-6506)

BRECK ALAN'S DELUXE TRIO
wed, may 10
8:30-11:30
@ little bear
(main st, evergreen)

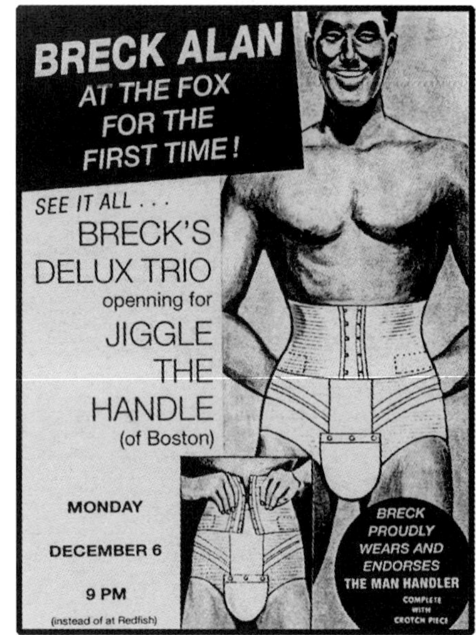
BRECK ALAN
AT THE FOX
FOR THE
FIRST TIME!
SEE IT ALL . . .
BRECK'S
DELUX TRIO
openning for
JIGGLE
THE
HANDLE
(of Boston)
MONDAY
DECEMBER 6
9 PM
(instead of at Redfish)
BRECK PROUDLY WEARS AND ENDORSES THE MAN HANDLER
COMPLETE WITH CROTCH PIECE

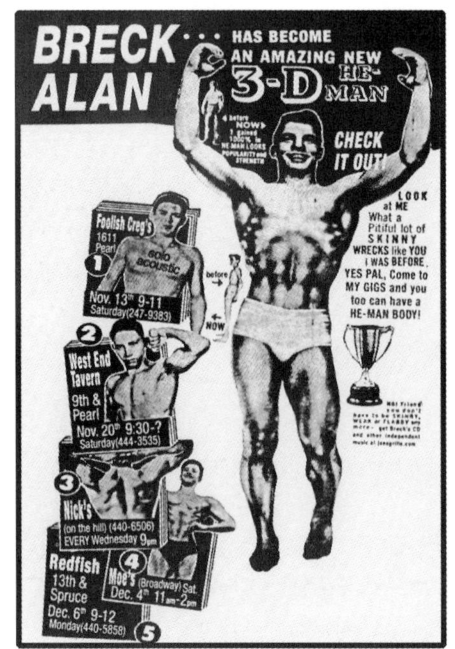
BRECK ALAN
... HAS BECOME AN AMAZING NEW 3-D HE-MAN
CHECK IT OUT!
LOOK at ME What a Pitiful lot of SKINNY WRECKS like YOU I WAS BEFORE, YES PAL, Come to MY GIGS and you too can have a HE-MAN BODY!
1
Foolish Craig's 1611 Pearl
solo acoustic
Nov. 13th 9-11 Saturday(247-9383)
2
West End Tavern 9th & Pearl
Nov. 20th 9:30-? Saturday(444-3535)
3
Nick's (on the hill) (440-6506) EVERY Wednesday 9pm
4
Moe's (Broadway) Sat. Dec. 4th 11am-2pm
Redfish 13th & Spruce Dec. 6th 9-12 Monday(440-5858)
5

The "Honey, I'm Home" gig
and
CD Release Party
The Breck Alan Band
January 25th,
10:00 p.m.
Nick's, Boulder
for more info, call joe's production & grille, inc.
442-1770
Come grind with Joe's to the edgy pop of Breck Alan's third release
Why Can't I

Let me first just say that I never set out to be a teacher. I took classes at various music schools and colleges around the world, as well as studying privately with a plethora of teachers for one reason: to learn what I needed to be a more productive singer. The problem was that when it came to vocal mechanics, that was no easy feat. Looking back, it still amazes me that so many teachers had so few tools, when it came to teaching vocal mechanics. It never seemed to take very long to expire a teacher of their knowledge of the specifics of the voice. I guess the only reason I felt I needed so many specifics, was that I never felt that I could cover all of the ground I wanted to cover with my singing. The things I had learned about it, hadn't taught me to continue my growth. So, consequently, I was always in search of more information that made sense to me. I was always experimenting with my own voice, just trying to do what every singer really wants to do, sound good to their own ear. I could never tell anyone that I haven't been strongly influenced by the world of information that exists on this subject called "Voice". What I can honestly say is that I feel *The Art of Body Singing* has fine tuned and organized the bits and pieces I picked up in one place or another. With some of it I got lucky and discovered on my own during my late night practice sessions over the last sixteen years. If I thought there was anything like this system of vocal mechanics training anywhere in the world, I can promise you that I would have bought it myself and surely not spent the five gillion hours producing this one. Although make no mistake, producing this system has been much like the entire journey of singing, a labor of love.

I owe, and am indebted for help along my vocal journey to many. A few of whom are Steve Heck and Peter Elvins for their huge patience in finally getting me to work hard enough to find my voice. To Richard Schumacher, Doug Alexander, Ran Blake and Don Rendal for their tenacity and insights in making me work my inner ear. To a myriad of other music teachers and musicians that I've been lucky enough to work with along the way who encouraged and inspired me. To Robert Cord, for rewarding me time and time again with praise, when I felt so overworked and underloved during my intense study years in Boston. To Joseph Nolan, for helping me build a vocal booth in my apartment in Boston, so that I could practice at all hours of the night without bothering my roommates, Laura and Kathleen. To Bob Minor, for the high praise of the first version of this project, and for encouraging me to finish this version. To every single one of the many students that I have been fortunate enough to work with, for it was only through working with this myriad of students (every one of them different) that I have been able to structure and fine tune *The Art of Body Singing*. And to Marina C. who told me once that all of my experiences good and bad would be portrayed in my singing, and I always thought that was a cool thing to say.

I must also credit here some of the vocal instruction publications that have strongly impressed and influenced me over the years. For starters, the first book about voice that I ever read was P. Mario Marafioti's "Caruso's Method of Voice Production" from Dover Press. This book had a profound influence over me and I still think its incredible. Another book that I've gained much pleasure from over the course of many years is "Your Voice at its Best" by David Blair McClosky. Mr. McClosky was a vocal therapist for many years in New England and has strongly influenced that field. His books are available through The Boston Music Company, 172 Tremont St., Boston, MA 02111. I also greatly enjoyed Alan Green's book, "The New Voice," largely because he spends the majority of the book dealing with matters concerning throat mechanics (a typically glossed over subject). Mr. Green's book is available through Hal Leonard Publishing. For matters concerning music interpretation, I strongly suggest H. Wesley Balk's books "The Complete Singer Actor" and "Performance Power" (available through University of Minnesota Press, Minneapolis 55414) and as a guide to diction I suggest "The Singers Manual of English Diction" by Madeleine Marshall (available on Schirmer Books). I must also say that I greatly admire Seth Riggs for his fresh ideas and huge influence on modern voice teaching.

Since finishing the writings in this book I have discovered the work of Lamperti and hope that I can say with all humility that he is a kindred spirit of mine. After you've worked your way through "The Art of Body Singing" check out Vocal Wisdom by Giovanni Battista Lamperti from Taplinger Publishing. It's beauty really shines once your sense of vocal mechanics are established.

Have Fun

Glossary

(This is the complete glossary for
The Art of Body Singing Volumes 1-4)

Adam's Apple: The front of your larynx. Technically your thyroid cartilage.

Adjusting on the Fly: An absolute necessity in performance to ensure that you maintain a continuous rather than a clunky and indecisive energy.

Air Spigot: The imagery of the control valve for the support system.

Anchoring: The art of placing your resonance at the nasal passage as an aid to control throat pressure and avoid oversinging. This should also be considered the beginning sound board for all resonance.

Anti-Constrictor Muscles: The muscles used in and around the throat (including the tongue) to drop the larynx, groove the tongue and open the throat.

Art of Body Singing: The system of vocal training which teaches you to intelligently navigate all of the components of the voice, guides you in the process of assembling and using your high quality instrument (voice), and prepares you for continued growth in singing and performance.

Assembly: The process of coordinating vocal techniques from actual vocal mechanics.

Auto Pilot Singing: Singing without the singer considering him/herself part of the audience. In other words, a singer that isn't listening to him/herself.

Back off: The thing singers guilty of oversinging have to constantly remind themselves to do. Big singing is done successfully by coordination, not bullying.

Backwards Into the Body: The art of singing behind and over the throat, using resonance to achieve size and color rather than force.

Belting Principle of Centering the Tone: Learning to eliminate the ease in, and attack the note in it's center. This increases projection value and gives the illusion of belting.

Blending: A common term for connecting the resonance chambers into a balanced tone. In this system we refer to blending as tone marriage, tone harmony and circle of tone.

Bottle Necking: Forcing too much air through the throat.

Bright Tone: 1. The result of singing a light, released tone (see throat pressure) and possibly singing through the mouth horn (see resonance). 2. The result of using the edgy overtones produced by the nasal horn to increase projection value (also see resonance).

Buffer Air: The airiness on top of the tone that acts as a release of throat pressure.

Bully: Something you can not successfully be with your voice. The voice is a democracy of all it's components.

Buzzy: Also called edgy, this is the resonance produced by the nasal horn.

The Candle Theory: The theory that states that no matter how big, or loud, or airy, or aggressive you may be singing, never should you be able to blow out a small candle placed in front of your mouth. Slightly flicker the candle, but never blow it out. Use your fingers as a gauge, not a candle.

Centering the Pitch: An exercise designed to help tune the ear for the result of having good intonation (being in tune).

Cloning the Tone: Staying loyal to a set tone for an extended period, for the purpose of mastering the techniques necessary to create that tone.

Closed Nasal Technique: Closing the nasal passage, resulting in a stuffy nose sound. This is a remarkable aid in learning to anchor your sound and not sing through the throat.

Clunkiness: Moving through the mechanics of voice in a not so seamless manner.

Coach: A provider of encouragement and generalisms. (as opposed to Teacher)

Connecting the Dots: The image of connecting the "four parts of the voice" in a balanced democracy.

Conscious Relaxation: The art of taking your awareness inside your throat and relaxing.

Constrictor Muscles: The muscles in the throat involved in swallowing and closing. One of the first things a singer must learn to do is identify and relax these muscles.

Continuous Energy: We don't sing notes, we sing phrases. You must supply continuous energy to a phrase to give it life. Do not ration your energy.

Conversation Level Throat Pressure: The perfect level of healthy throat pressure, that should never be exceeded regardless of size or energy level of singing.

Crescendo: A dynamic change from softest to loudest.

Deceptive Air: See fast air.

Decrescendo: A dynamic change from loudest to softest.

Diction: In this system we stress skipping off the consonant and living on the vowel. More specifics are certainly mentioned in each volume but an extensive study of diction with a dedicated diction manual is suggested.

Diphthong: A sound composed of two consecutive vowel sounds in the same syllable.

Double Hand Technique: One hand on the chest to be constantly in touch with the resonance being produced there, and the other hand on the lower abdominals to gently remind (not push) them to stay awake.

Drool Exercise: The exercise in which we learn to relax so effectively in and around the throat, that we kick in the salivatory glands.

Dropped Larynx Technique: Using the anti-constrictor muscles in the throat to drop the larynx, this technique is used to both change the shape of this area in the throat (different shape equals different tonal characteristics), and to help with placing chest resonance.

Dynamic Breathing: Developing a sense of dynamic range (from the quietest and softest to the loudest and hardest) in your singing. This is achieved not only with a good sense of singing mechanics, but also with good grasp of energy changes.

Ease In and Ease Out Techniques: The art of eliminating the clunkiness often associated with entering and exiting a note by easing in and easing out.

Ease: The state of being a singer should be in, while learning to coordinate the first two volumes of The Art of Body Singing.

Energy Air: See fast air.

Energy: A wonderful, variable, necessary part of singing.

Entries: Entering a note.

Exaggeration: A necessity in the practice room in order to thoroughly discover the instrument.

Experimenting: Something of paramount importance in truly navigating the mechanics of the voice. Experimenting though, without good guidance from a good mechanics teacher typically leads to a plethora of bad and unhealthy singing habits.

Extreme Reverse Resonance Exercise: An exercise where you practice pulling your resonance in the opposite direction from which the pitch is traveling.

Falsetto Principles: 1. In this system falsetto is described as the tone created by singing through the mouth horn. 2. The light, bright voice produced by disconnecting (releasing) from the chest and nasal horn resonance chambers and singing exclusively in the mouth horn.

Fast Air: The technique designed to increase the level of energy (air) in singing without increasing throat pressure.

Fast Air Crescendos: This technique involves a ratio shift from a number three ratio with fast air energy to a number one ratio, without changing the energy. This should produce the largest possible size in your tone.

Feel: One part of singing that makes the journey so fun is feeling all of the components of the voice in your body at work together. This is not about manipulation, but about awareness.

Finishing Out: The term used for intentionally or unintentionally withdrawing from an isolated tone.

The Four Parts to a Singing Session: Preliminary warm-up, exercise/workout period, warm-up singing, full singing.

The Fluttering Exercise: The exercise used for centering the pitch.

Flowering: The effect of tone marriage taking shape and increasing your circle of tone.

Freedom: A result of being open.

Grooved Tongue Position: Lying the tongue flat on the floor of the mouth and grooving it so that the tone passage is unobstructed to the exit of the mouth.

Growth: The thing that happens when one stays "open" and nurses one's talents on an ongoing basis.

Gushing: A random release of air during phonation.

Half Way Technique: The beginning of tone marriage, this technique combines the advantages of anchoring with the closed nasal technique, along with adding body to your sound with the chest tone.

Heroes: The singers that should be slightly out of your reach, and therefore inspire you to keep raising the height of the bar during your workouts.

High Sigh: A tone isolation exercise focusing on the mouth horn while swooping downward from the upper range to the lower range.

Inner Ear: The first part of the voice, this is your guide to good musicianship (i.e. pitch, note choice, rhythm etc.) and instrument specific recognition (i.e. tone, inflection, volume, attitude, etc.).

Inside Your Body: Where the mechanics of your instrument live, and therefore where you must take your sensibilities so that you may feel these mechanics at work.

Internal Tachometer: The gauge connected to the series of singing mechanics that prevents you from oversinging even when you're not hearing yourself on the level you might like to.

Interpretation: The art of finding the right colors in your tone and expression to sell the meaning of whatever you are singing. Singing is after all, a form of acting.

Intonation: The result of an instrument being in tune when played.

Journey: Something you must be willing to take if you are serious about finding "your voice."

Kick Start Technique: The technique where the hands are cupped three or four inches below the naval to gentle stimulate the lower abdominal muscles during the "Way Down Exercise."

Larynx: The temple of the vocal cords.

Learning Curve: Something you should expect to encounter before the high level singing techniques taught in this system become natural.

Looping: The wonderful technique of repeating a small section of something over and over until it is right before moving on.

Magic Wand: The thing most singers wish I had so they wouldn't have to practice. One session $5,000, good-bye.

Masque: See open nasal anchor in this glossary.

Mechanical Switch: Often referred to in this system as switches, and turning on the switches. These are the mechanics of your instrument that you must learn to turn on and develop in your warm-up and vocal workout so that they are available to you during singing.

Minimal Mouth Movement: The art of learning to articulate first inside your mouth with the help of your ear. Excessive mouth movement leads to tension.

Mirror: The thing that can save you a lot of time in learning vocal technique.

The Mixo Exercise: An endurance exercise used with the lip roll.

Mouth Sizing: A common sense technique of opening your mouth wider (still using the singer's smile) as the energy level (air level) increases.

Multi-Register Singing: An obvious breaking of registers as the pitch moves from one area of a singers range to another. Your first goal in this system is one register singing. Then, if you choose to break registers for reasons of interpretation, it will be from choice, not default.

Muscle Memory Singing: The result of typical voice coaching and learning via imitation as opposed to learning via mechanics training. This is the sort of singing that sounds the same on every song regardless of the song's meaning or intention.

Nasal Horn Buzz: The tone isolation exercise used to place resonance deeper and deeper into the nasal horn by maintaining a very open nasal passage.

Naturalization: One of the first keys in stripping away old singy habits and cultivating a new foundation from which to grow. A good place to start is with speaking the melody.

No Black Sheep Rule: The art of listening to your practice so that complete control and evenness of your exercises can be attained. From that foundation, more expressive unevenness in singing will be within your grasp.

No Note District: The complete bottom or top of one's singing range.

Number Two Crescendos: Crescendos done from start to finish on a number two ratio. This requires a good sense of energy changes.

Old School Flex: The endearing technique taught in days of old to flex your buttocks while singing extremely difficult passages. As strange as it may be, it has it's place.

Olympic Level Singing: The high level, high energy singing that ambitious singers aspire to.

One Breath Exercise: A tone exercise used for endurance and distance training (the notes being at different distances apart).

One Register Singing: The art of keeping the tone connected while singing throughout your range (as opposed to multi-register singing).

Open Body Vibrato: Open body vibrato is the result of balancing the echoing between the resonance chambers, the evenness of the support system and the perfect level of throat pressure.

Open Nasal Anchor: The nasal passage (where the uvula lives) is the first place the air and initial tone from the vocal cords make contact. By centering (placing) the beginning of resonance here, we can control the pressure in the throat and begin the flowering process of tone marriage. "LET THE BUZZ BE THE GUIDE." This is what is referred to in classical teachings as singing in the "masque."

Open Rib Cage Technique: This technique involves keeping your sternum high and your rib cage open with the aid of the "intercostal muscles" during singing.

Open: Open body, open throat, open mind.

Overcompensating: Using too much air to "reach" a note (usually most apparent in the upper range) resulting in oversinging.

Overpressurizing: What happens in the throat when constriction and pushing are the habits of a singer.

Oversinging: A product of trying to "bully" singing rather than coordinate it. The result is poor tone quality and vocal strain.

Overtones: Sometimes called harmonics, these are the series of tones that effectively harmonize with the fundamental tone being produced. These overtones are what gives each instrument it's unique color and quality (timbre).

Percentage Technique: This involves opening up the nasal passage while practicing the half way technique to finish off the circle of tone.

Phonation: Producing sound with the voice.

Ping Pong Exercise: An exercise used first for ear training, and secondly as a distance exercise for singing.

Po Pa Exercise: A high energy distance exercise taught in volume three.

Posture: Posture is about aligning and freeing up your body so that it may contribute to, rather than hinder, your singing.

Potential: Whatever you're willing to make it.

Practice: Often referred to as "wood shedding" by musicians, this slight inconvenience will only entirely determine your success in this (and just about any other) field.

Professional: Officially someone who gets paid for what they do, but realistically one who aspires to the attitude and competence of professionalism.

Projection: For your singing to literally fly from your mouth and body to the listener.

Pulsing Projection: An emphasis exercise designed to give life and expression to your singing performance.

Ratios: See three air ratios.

Ratio Shifting: The practice of shifting seamlessly from one ratio to another.

Rationing: Supplying your singing with rations of support rather than continuous energy.

Resonance: The sympathetic vibration of your body to the tiny vibrations that begin in the throat.

Resonance Follows Pitch: During auto pilot singing your resonance placement will automatically follow your pitch around like a little puppy (i.e. when you're singing in your upper range the resonance will be up in your head, and when you're singing in your lower range the resonance will be in down in your body). The result of this is multi register singing.

Resonance Placement: Placement is often described as "placing" your resonance in your head or chest etc. To me, the key to placement is the "anchor." After that it's really about opening up and attaching the other resonances in your body to this.

Resonance Shifting: The exercise of vertically shifting from one resonance chamber to another (mouth horn to chest, back to mouth horn, then into the nasal horn and back to mouth horn).

Reverse Resonance Psychology: The practice of pulling back and down with your resonance placement as you ascend in pitch, and pulling up with your resonance placement as you descend in pitch.

Routine: The methodical series of events that should warm you up, work you out, and put you on the path to continued growth.

Rushing the Tone: Singing through the throat as a result of not having the patience to sing backwards into the body to rely on resonance for size and color.

Santa Ho Ho: An exercise to stimulate the lower abdominal muscles into action. After these muscles have begun to respond it is important to work back towards using them on a reflex basis.

Scorching: A burning irritation in the throat associated with oversinging.

Scratch Tape: A tape used to listen back to yourself practicing exercises and singing.

Set-up: 1. The physical feelings you should teach yourself to feel inside your body before phonation begins. 2. The feelings you must feel in the throat before attacking a note without the ease-in technique.

Settling: That period when all things learned must settle into your mind, body and spirit so that they might surface in a usable form.

Seven Points of Relaxation: Down the face, jaw hinge, stretch jaw, root of tongue, horizontal larynx, back of head and neck, shoulders.

Silent Singing: Just that, singing in your mind.

Singer Release: This effect is achieved by releasing into the mouth horn from a more connected tone.

Singer's Smile: The shaping of the mouth into a slight smile to create a slightly larger exit for cleaner purer articulation.

Singing an Octave Below the Melody: A good way to work your bottom range, wake up your ear and possibly help sing in a relaxed manner in the car.

Singing Backwards Into Your Body: The art of singing behind your throat and using resonance, support and good anchoring instead of force to achieve high level singing.

Singing Behind Your Throat: The art of singing with the perfect level of throat pressure. This is sometimes referred to as singing over your throat.

Singing Off the Breath: Never holding your breath before beginning to sing. This principle also applies to not allowing yourself to constrict in the throat should support begin to diminish.

Singing Through the Throat: The act of creating too much throat pressure (over-pressurization) from either constricting in the throat, pushing, or not anchoring well.

Singy: The weird singing quality many singers possess when trying to sing beyond their capabilities before learning to do so. This often involves trying to imitate opera singers or pop singers, the result being one of a comic nature.

Siren: A swooping, ascending exercise, staying locked into the half way technique.

Speaking the Melody: The technique that should teach you to clearly understand the connection between singing and speaking.

Strain: A product of oversinging.

Student: Anyone hungry to learn something and willing to go through the necessary steps to reach that goal.

Style: Ideally, the reflection of the individual's personality and life experience, which should be thoroughly enhanced (not manipulated) through vocal training.

Support System: All that is connected with breath control in singing.

Supposedly Tone Deaf: Although I'm sure it's possible that a physical or psychological defect in a small percentage of people might cause the disability to discern and match pitches, In all of my cases I have never seen this to be so. People who cannot match pitches simply need to be taught to do so in a gentle methodical manner (see Volume One "Before We Get Started").

Sustain: To hold a note (on a vowel or musical consonant) for a duration longer than is done during speaking. In fact sustaining is the first departure from speaking into singing.

Sustained Tone Combos: A good way to practice sustained tones while changing through a variety mechanical techniques.

System: An organized methodology for learning anything.

Tangible: That which we can really learn to identify, hear, feel and often see, as opposed to the pure imagery that is so often used in teaching this instrument. Certainly not to suggest that all imagery is useless.

Taps Exercise: A light vocal cord massage used for light rehabilitation of vocal strain and as a wonderful warm down.

Teacher: A provider of realism and hard cold facts, while maintaining the insights to help a student find his/her individual path.

Tessetura: The part of the singing range (middle), which produces the highest quality level for the least amount of effort.

Thoracic Pressure: The valvular process of constricting within the larynx to trap air in the lungs. This is done with the aid of the intrinsic muscles of the larynx and the ventricular bands (often referred to as "false vocal chords").

Three Air Ratios: The subject that not only allows us to understand how air works under the tone, but on top of the tone as well. Also a wonderful tool for understanding throat pressure.

Three Parts to a Note: The beginning, the middle and the end. Practicing the ease in and ease out techniques is a good way to truly understand the three parts to a note and to eliminate clunkiness in singing.

Three Resonance Chambers: Chest, mouth horn and nasal horn.

Three Steps to Working Out a Difficult Passage: Happy throat, placement, size.

Three Ways to Crescendo: Shift towards a less airy ratio, increase your energy level, increase your circle of tone.

Throat: This is where everything begins in singing. Although the voice is a democracy of it's four components (inner ear, throat, support system and resonance) great reverence must be paid to this part of your instrument to maintain good vocal health and good tone.

Throat Effects: The technique used to healthily create those tones ranging from the lightly smoky to the heavily grindy.

Throat Management: The art of relaxing the constrictor muscles, using the anti-constrictor muscles correctly and monitoring throat pressure.

Throat Pressure: The pressure created between the vocal cords and the respiratory system during phonation.

Throat Rattle or Throat Distortion: The rattling of phlegm in the throat as a result of singing through the throat as opposed to singing over and behind the throat.

Tone by Attitude: A performance exercise designed to help you connect the various tones you've been working on with various attitudes and emotions.

Tone Isolation Exercises: Isolating your resonance in one resonance chamber at a time.

Tone Marriage: Also referred to as tone harmony and circle of tone, this is the art of uniting the resonance chambers to create a whole (tone) larger than the sum of it's parts.

Tone Passage: The passage in the throat from where voice begins (vocal cords) to where it exits (the mouth and nasal passage). This is technically referred to as the Pharynx.

Tone Variety: The art of tapping into different tones as they relate to the interpretation of singing.

Tongue Roll and Lip Roll Exercises: Wonderful mechanics exercises taught in this system to teach you to sing behind the pressure created by rolling the tongue or lips, instead of through that pressure. Also wonderful exercises for developing the air spigot in the support system.

Tongue Roll Mm Ah and Lip Roll Mm Ah Exercises: The mechanical exercises designed to help you coordinate the transition from the Tongue Roll or Lip Roll, to a hum and then to an open vowel tone.

Tool Songs: Memorized songs of the appropriate difficulty level for a singer to practice various techniques over.

Triphthong: Three connected vowel sounds.

Two Parts to the Middle: The technique of changing your tone in the middle of a vowel as a highlight or expression.

Under Compensating: Using too little air to reach a note (common in both upper and lower ranges) resulting in tone loss or throat constriction.

Unfinished Tone: Another term for an isolated tone.

Upper Middle: The area in your singing range above a typical singers vocal break. This is the most projecting area of your range, and typically the most difficult to convincingly develop.

Uvula: The cone shaped projection hanging above the back of the tongue. The uvula is a good guide when learning to switch back and forth from an open to closed nasal passage. When the uvula is low the nasopharynx (which leads into the nasal passage) is open. When the uvula is high this passage is closed.

Vertical Resonance: Before you can successfully navigate the art of tone marriage you should be able to place your resonance in each resonance chamber individually (moving up and down). This is referred to as thinking vertically in your resonance.

Vibrato Principles: Open body vibrato is the goal in this system. See open body vibrato in this glossary.

Vocabulary: Officially "all of the words of a language." The Art of Body Singing was designed using as much everyday language as possible to articulate the specific world of voice training.

Vocal Break: Generally the result of disconnecting from the resonance chambers that produce the most size and volume (chest and nasal horn) and releasing into the mouth horn.

Vocal Cords: Coupled with air from the support system, the tiny vibrations started by the vocal cords (also called vocal folds) are where it all begins in singing.

Vocal Disorders: A direct result of over-pressurization in the throat.

Vocal Fatigue: The result of overpressurizing the vocal cords and larynx, resulting in a weak and tired voice.

Vocal Hygiene: The art of maintaining a healthy singing voice at all times.

Vocal Mechanics: All of the tangible physical components of the voice (i.e.. throat, support system and resonance, which are of course guided by the ear).

Vocal Techniques: The skills required to fluidly and consistently navigate the mechanics of the voice.

Vocal Therapy: The various procedures used to correct vocal disorders due to oversinging. Everything about The Art of Body Singing teaches prevention of vocal disorders so that correction and therapy should, hopefully, never be needed.

Volume Diamond: There is a place in your middle range that will produce your loudest singing volume. From that point the volume will taper in both directions. Projection can, however, effectively disguise that tapering.

Warm-up: An imperative for the healthy, professional singer. This is how we turn on all of the mechanical switches for our voice so that they are available to us during singing.

Warming Down: A good idea after high level singing to prevent swelling in the throat due to the high blood circulation created in that area.

Wave of Energy: The imagery used to describe the energy in singing as a wave leaving the entire body, and the notes and words as ships on top of that wave.

Way Down Exercise: The exercise that helps us focus on using our lower support system, begin the process of singing in our lower range, and maintain our big body posture.

Work Out: The part of the singing session that yields the highest level warm-up as well as the highest level of growth.

Yawning the Adam's Apple Down: An often taught exercise to teach singers to drop the larynx.